How to Analyze Jobs

A Step-by-Step Approach

BUSINESS & LEGAL REPORTS, INC.
39 Academy Street, Madison, CT 06443-1513

EDITORIAL AND PRODUCTION STAFF:

Assistant Editor: Judith A. Ruddy
Editorial Assistant: Beverly M. Eggert
Design: John F. Kallio
Design Assistants: Lisa Aumuller, Judy Fettig

© 1982 BUSINESS & LEGAL REPORTS, INC.
Reprinted in 1993
Fourth printing

All rights reserved. This book may not be reproduced in part or in whole by any process without written permission from the publisher, except as noted below.

Authorization to photocopy items for internal or personal use or the internal or personal use of specific clients is granted by Business & Legal Reports, Inc., provided that the base fee of U.S. $0 per copy, plus U.S. $0.50 per page is paid directly to Copyright Clearance Center, 27 Congress Street, Salem, MA 01970, USA. For those organizations that have been granted a photocopy license by CCC, a separate system of payment has been arranged. The fee code for users of the Transactional Reporting Service is: 1-55645-402-3/82/$0+$.50.

ISBN 1-55645-402-3

Printed in the United States of America

Job Descriptions under the Americans with Disabilities Act (ADA)

Employers covered by the Americans with Disabilities Act know by now that they may have some special obligations with respect to job analysis and descriptions.

Under the ADA, an employer cannot discriminate against an individual who can perform the "essential functions" of the job in question, with or without reasonable accommodation. "Essential functions" are those duties that an individual *must* be able to perform, i.e., fundamental rather than marginal duties, and this is where job analysis and descriptions come in.

In determining whether a function is essential, one of the things that the Equal Employment Opportunity Commission (EEOC) will look at is a written job description prepared by the employer before advertising the position or interviewing applicants. Job descriptions are not required by the ADA, and some employers may decide not to develop them. But for most employers, detailing the essential functions in a job description will help ensure that disabled applicants are not rejected because they cannot perform marginal job duties.

When is a particular job duty an "essential function"? According to the EEOC guidelines, this inquiry focuses first on whether the employer actually requires employees in the position to perform the particular function. For example, if an employer says that typing is an essential function, but has never required any employee in the position to type, this will be evidence that typing is not, in fact, an essential function.

If individuals who hold the position are actually required to perform the function, then the function may be considered essential for any one of several reasons, among them:

- The position exists to perform the function in question. For example, when an individual is hired to proofread documents, the ability to proofread is an essential function because this is the only reason the position exists.

- The employer has a limited number of employees among whom the function can be distributed. If an employer has a small number of employees and a wide variety of work that has to be done, it may be necessary for each employee to perform a variety of functions. The options for reorganizing the work may be more limited than they would be in a large organization. In this type of situation, functions may become essential that might not be considered essential if there were a larger staff.

- The function is highly specialized. In certain professions and highly skilled positions, an employer may hire an employee because of his or her special expertise or ability to perform a particular function. The performance of that specialized task would be an essential function.

In meeting your obligations under the ADA, give some thought to what the EEOC guidelines say, and follow these additional tips from the experts when doing job analysis and developing your job descriptions:

- Use the term "essential functions"

- Make sure to focus on *what* is to be accomplished, not *how*, i.e., don't assume that there's only one way to do a job

- Combine the input of several employees and managers

- Review job descriptions with employees and document their agreement

- Update your job descriptions on a regular basis to reflect changes.

For more detailed instruction concerning your obligations under the Americans with Disabilities Act, consult BLR's book *How to Comply with the Americans with Disabilities Act*.

CONTENTS

Chapter One: What Is Job Analysis? 1
- What is analyzed? . . . 2
- When should jobs be analyzed? . . . 3
- Who must be involved? . . . 4

Chapter Two: The Job Analyst 6
- An overview . . . 8

Chapter Three: Uses of Job Analysis 10
- Job analysis program survey . . . 12

Chapter Four: Preparing for Job Analysis 14
- Presentation of information . . . 15
- Determining objectives . . . 16
- Developing materials . . . 17
- Checklist for job analysis forms design . . . 18
- Sample organization charts . . . 21
- Identifying benchmark jobs . . . 23
- Selecting and training the analyst . . . 24
- Introducing the participants . . . 24
- The U.S.D.O.L. Handbook . . . 26
- Sample form . . . 30

Chapter Five: Methods and Techniques 34
- Job analysis information sheet . . . 36
- Which method is best for you? . . . 41
- The Air Force comparison . . . 42

(Continued)

- Observation technique . . . 43
- Interview technique . . . 45
- Sample interview forms . . . 51, 55, 56, 58
- Questionnaire method . . . 63
- Sample questionnaire . . . 66, 70, 72
- Functional job analysis . . . 76
- Task inventories . . . 77
- Critical incident technique . . . 77
- Position analysis questionnaire . . . 78
- The Hay System . . . 79
- Job Information Matrix System . . . 80
- Job element method . . . 80
- Occupational analysis inventory . . . 81
- Why are so many companies dissatisfied? . . . 81

What Is 'Job Analysis'?

Before two jobs can be compared on any basis at all, you have to know the following: 1) the component parts that, added together, make each job what it is; 2) how its various elements are similar to the basic components of other jobs in the organization; and 3) how its elements differ from other jobs. In short, its content must be analyzed. "Job analysis" is the process of obtaining information about a particular job in order to establish a basis for accurately describing it and for determining its specifications and requirements.

This process typically occurs in two stages, the first being to elicit the information from a source—for example, by interviewing a job incumbent. The second stage is to organize and present the information that has been obtained in a useful format—usually a conventional job description. It is difficult to separate the two stages because each depends heavily on the other for its meaning and usefulness. That is, the data collected during job analysis has little value until it is organized and presented in a meaningful form. Similarly, a good job description *must* be the result of a thorough job analysis or it cannot be depended upon as an objective source of job information.

Job analysis is concerned with facts—with information about the *job* and not the incumbent. It should therefore be distinguished from a related term, "worker analysis," which focuses attention on the employee's characteristics through the use of physical examinations, tests, interviews, and other procedures. It should also be distinguished from "job classification," which is the process of categorizing jobs according to the type of work being performed, the skill required, or other job-related factors. Job classification is normally linked to wage and salary administration, while job analysis can be put to broader use.

When we say that job analysis should focus on the job and not on the incumbent, we do not mean that the skills, knowledge, and aptitudes a worker must possess in order to perform the job successfully should be overlooked entirely. But there is an important difference between what is required of the worker in terms of aptitudes, skills, and personal traits, and the particular behavioral qualities of the individual currently filling the position in question. The emphasis in job analysis should be on the former, not the latter. This information can then be translated into job specifications. (Job descriptions are the subject of another book in this series, "How to Write Job Descriptions.")

WHAT IS ANALYZED?

The job analysis process seeks to provide information in seven major areas, each of which is described briefly below:

(1) **Work activities.** This covers what the worker does—specific tasks that make up the job assignment; their relative timing and importance; the simplicity or complexity of tasks; and responsibility for other workers, for property, or for funds. The focus here is on *what* is done.

(2) **The job context.** This includes the job's location, physical setting, and working conditions; supervision received or exercised; union jurisdiction (if any); work schedule; and financial and nonfinancial incentives.

(3) **Tools, machines, equipment and work aids used.** For example, does the worker deal with lathes, milling machines, punch presses, electronic ignition testers, or micrometers?

(4) **How the job is performed.** The emphasis here is on the nature of operations—feeding, removing, drilling, setting up, etc. Some job analysis systems (but not all) also develop work standards and work measurements, such as time taken for a particular task.

(5) **The personnel requirements for the job.** This includes experience, education, training, physical demands, coordination or dexterity, mental capabilities, aptitudes, and social skills.

(6) **Job relationships.** This covers not only the guidance and supervision received and/or exercised, but also the advancement opportunities, patterns of promotion, cooperation received, and the usual sources of employees for the job.

(7) **Job-related tangibles or intangibles.** This includes the materials processed, the knowledge dealt with or applied (as in accounting) and the products made or services performed.

Jobs should be analyzed *as they exist* at the time the analysis is performed—not as they should exist, not as they have existed in the past, and not as they exist in similar organizations. If the job analysis and the resulting job description do not reflect the reality of the job, there is little point in going through the process.

WHEN SHOULD JOBS BE ANALYZED?

There are a number of events that might trigger the need for job analysis, and recent court decisions in the field of comparable worth is only one of them. Union representatives may demand a revision of job descriptions to reflect more accurately the work performed; this would naturally entail a new job analysis as well. The recent flood of legislative mandates to develop nondiscriminatory employment standards has also boosted job analysis efforts. Some firms have undertaken job analysis when it has been brought to their attention that certain employees (primarily women and minorities) have been barred from certain jobs by duties that are unrelated to primary job content or that are significantly more demanding than the normal job duties. Job analysis brings these and other inequities to the surface, where they can be dealt with in a constructive manner.

Of course, good management practice dictates that a periodic review of job content can nip a number of personnel problems in the bud. When employees know what is expected of them and management knows what they are doing, misunderstandings and conflicts about job duties and performance standards are kept to a minimum. Job analysis also forces management to reconsider the qualifications that employees must bring to a job in light of the duties and responsibilities they will be expected to carry out once they have been hired or promoted. Where discrepancies are uncovered, immediate action can be taken to bring job specifications in line with these duties, and complaints of comparable worth violations or unfair employment practices can be headed off long before they land an employer in court.

Whatever the motivation for instituting a job analysis program, there are some essential preliminary considerations. Remember that the activities involved in gathering, analyzing, and recording information on job content demand time, money, and manpower; it is not an effort that should be undertaken lightly or without considerable forethought. Ask yourself these questions:

- Does top management understand what a job analysis program entails? Are they willing to commit the required time, money, and manpower?
- Do company managers and supervisors understand that changes may be recommended as a result of the analysis? Do they realize how such changes might affect them and their employees?
- If job analysis has been undertaken in the past, what were the results? No action? actions that undermined the job security or career development of managers or their subordinates? If past results were nonexistent or negative, the attitude of the work force to a renewed job analysis effort can hardly be expected to be enthusiastic.
- What kind of cooperation can be expected from employees? What orientation efforts have been (or could be) made to acquaint the work force with the job analysis process and to enlist their support ahead of time?

If you are approaching job analysis for the first time, you probably won't be able to answer many of these questions at this point. But it's a good idea to keep them in mind as you read the sections that follow—and you *should* have answers for all of them before you actually implement your job analysis program.

WHO MUST BE INVOLVED IN THE PROGRAM?

Since job analysis and the writing of job descriptions usually go hand-in-hand, participation in the program must be broad-based. Several groups and individuals will play significant roles—top management, supervisory management, the job analyst, the consultant (if one is used), employees, and of course the union (if one or more is present). The role of each of these groups is outlined briefly below:

I. The role of general management is to:
    A. Establish the need for a program;
    B. Issue policy statements, directives, and other communications;
    C. Delegate authority for carrying out various aspects of the program;
    D. Establish a time frame for program implementation;
    E. Resolve conflicts;
    F. Provide continuing support;
    G. Either appoint or carry out review and approval procedures.

II. The role of supervisory management is to:
    A. Implement the program;
    B. Participate in job analysis;
    C. Communicate with employees concerning the program;
    D. Review and approve the results.

III. The role of the job analyst is to:
    A. Develop data-gathering methods;
    B. Gather data and analyze results;
    C. Study and develop compensable factors;
    D. Prepare or participate in the drafting of job descriptions;
    F. Chair or coordinate committee work:
    G. Participate in union negotiations.

IV. The employee's role is to:
    A. Participate in data-gathering;
    B. Participate in the drafting of job descriptions (if company policy permits);
    C. Participate in review committees (if company policy permits).

V. The union's role is to:
    A. Support data-gathering (through its members);
    B. Appoint representatives to work with the job analyst;
    C. Participate in review and approval procedures;
    D. Participate in drafting job descriptions;
    E. Negotiate with management.

VI. The role of the consultant is to:
    A. Advise management on the need for a program, communications concerning the program, and audit and review procedures.

B. Advise or work with the job analyst in the following areas:
1. data gathering and analysis
2. writing job descriptions
3. meeting statutory requirements
4. establishing systematic procedures.
C. Participate in the development of other phases of wage and salary administration (job evaluation, job pricing, etc.).

Even from this rather sketchy outline of duties and responsibilities, it is easy to see that a job analysis and job description program extends to every level of the company hierarchy and requires the support and cooperation of every individual. This list of responsibilities will grow as you actually get involved in setting up your own program, but it can serve as a helpful eye-opener to see at a glance the magnitude of the effort involved.

The Job Analyst

The major factors to be considered in selecting people to act as job analysts are formal education, previous work experience, and personal qualifications. As far as education is concerned, the analyst should have a college degree (or its equivalent) either in industrial engineering or in business administration, with a major in industrial management. A broad exposure to various types of work is of equal importance. This combination of formal education and work experience is valuable because it helps the analyst appreciate how jobs are designed and how work is organized. It gives him or her an understanding of specialized job terminology and the significance of the facts picked up in the course of job analysis.

As far as personal qualifications are concerned, the job analyst's role involves extensive contacts with all types of people at all levels in the company and in a wide variety of situations. Since job information is most commonly gathered through observation and interview, the analyst must be able to establish immediate rapport with employees, so that his or her questions will not irritate or arouse unwarranted suspicion. But it is equally important that the analyst maintain a certain "distance," so that emotions do not interfere with the objectivity that is so essential. He must be able to inspire the confidence of supervisors, employees, and union representatives in his ability to be fair and to understand the significance of the information he obtains.

Finally, the job analyst must possess some writing ability so that she can prepare a narrative statement (or job description) that is clear, concise, and free from redundancy. She should also be able to use descriptive phrases that will facilitate comparisons with other jobs. By "writing ability" we do not mean that the analyst should have a distinctive writing style, since job descriptions tend to follow a predetermined format.

A competent job analyst knows what to look for in the job. She avoids injecting her own opinions—for example, stating that a particular job is "boring" or that certain working conditions are "ideal." She studiously avoids analyzing the employee rather than the job, because she is fully aware that many of the employee's personal traits may have no relevance whatsoever to the behavior that is required on the job. Above all, she knows how to distinguish between crucial tasks and those that are merely incidental in the performance of the job.

In what other areas must the job analyst excel? He must have demonstrated competence in the following areas:

1. **Work planning:** The job analyst must know how to organize the various aspects of the program while at the same time maintaining the flexibility to accommodate necessary changes.
2. **Program knowledge:** He must maintain open and continuing communications with supervisors and managers who are involved in the program so that he can keep abreast of their progress and problems.
3. **Fact finding:** He must have an in-depth knowledge of the various data-gathering techniques, and skill in applying them as needed.
4. **Coordinating with other specialists:** The job analyst must work closely with other personnel specialists. The person who is only interested in "running his own show" is not cut out for the job analyst's role.
5. **Keeping supervisors informed:** He is expected to recognize when advice and assistance from his superior is necessary, and to keep this individual informed on the program's progress. However, as a specialist, the analyst is also expected to recommend the best course of action to take when problems are referred to upper management.
6. **Judgment:** Good judgment must be exercised at all times. This extends to avoiding inter-department feuds, belittling or inflating the job, appearing to have a closed mind, being unnecessarily arbitrary, etc.
7. **Loyalty:** It goes almost without saying that the job analyst is expected to be loyal to the personnel department and to his superior, to support their policies and decisions, and to avoid discussing with other individuals any disagreements arising within the job analysis program.

Very few companies employ persons for the sole purpose of analyzing jobs and writing job descriptions. The job analyst, therefore, is usually a specialist within the personnel department, and may also be known as a "compensation specialist" or some other title indicating a broader range of responsibilities.

AN OVERVIEW OF THE JOB ANALYSIS PROCESS

What do job analysts actually do? The obvious answer here is that they conduct job analyses. But before we get into a detailed discussion of the various job analysis techniques, it is important that we take a look at the seven basic steps the job analyst must follow in carrying out his or her role.

(1) *Determine how the information collected during job analysis will be used.* The scope of the job analysis effort depends on the reasons for which it is being conducted (see the following section on "Uses of Job Analysis"). Determining exactly what purpose(s) the information collected will serve is something that job analysts must do in cooperation with top management and their superior(s) within the personnel department.

(2) *Select the appropriate sources of job information.* This includes not only deciding what individuals (supervisors, department heads, line workers, etc.) will be asked to contribute job information but also what data-gathering techniques will be used. A careful study of the organizational chart (if it is up-to-date) can help clarify the relationships between individual jobholders and those who are responsible for their performance. It is usually recommended that a number of sources—for example, the employee, his supervisor, and the department head—be tapped for information on a particular job so that the most objective possible picture of the job can be developed.

(3) *Develop a budget and timetable.* The number of people who will be involved in the effort, the required knowledge, and the time necessary to perform the analyses are the primary cost factors to be considered. If a consultant is being used, this would be an additional cost to figure in. The job analyst also has to select benchmark jobs (those that will be analyzed first) and set up a schedule that meets with the approval of all those concerned.

(4) *Determine how the job should be performed.* The point has already been made that job analysis should attempt to describe the job *as it exists*. But what if the current jobholder is not performing the tasks as expected by his or her superior? A job description based on a job analysis that reflects substandard performance by an incumbent is of little use to the organization in such areas as orientation, compensation, recruiting, or legal compliance. This is why it is important for the job analyst to know ahead of time what *should* be happening in a particular job. Even though the analyst's goal is to record the job as it exists, it is important for him to draw attention to situations where there is a significant deviation between desired and actual performance.

(5) *Study the job as it is being performed.* This is the step that most of us identify with the term "job analysis." It involves soliciting information through specific job analysis techniques and then developing clear, concise, accurate statements describing the duties performed by the employee. The job analyst reports the job exactly as it is being performed.

(6) *Clarify discrepancies.* When there is a discrepancy between desired performance and the way the job is actually being performed, analysts must double-check their findings with someone else—usually the jobholder's superior. Such discrepancies might be the result of insufficient instruction or training. They might also reflect the inadequacies of past job descriptions. For example, the old job description might have included certain duties simply to justify a higher pay rate, when in fact these duties are either unnecessary or seldom required.

(7) *Review the information with employees and supervisors.* Both the incumbent and the immediate supervisor must be given an opportunity to review the final analysis to determine whether it is accurate, easily understood, and comprehensive enough to provide all the information needed for a job description. The review procedure not only promotes accuracy but also encourages employee acceptance of the program.

This brief overview of the job analysis process focuses on the role played by the job analyst. Each of these steps will be enlarged upon in the pages that follow, but you should try to maintain a sense of the analyst's contribution to every phase of the job analysis program and the corresponding importance of finding someone who is capable of fulfilling this vital role.

3

Uses Of Job Analysis

The information gathered during job analysis serves a wide variety of purposes, most of which mesh tightly with the uses of the resulting job descriptions. A study conducted several years ago revealed that the most widespread use was in recruitment and selection, followed closely by the setting of equitable wage and salary levels. But the development since then of more sophisticated data-gathering techniques has led in turn to a wider variety of uses for the resulting information. The list below, adapted from a survey of national job analysis methods, summarizes some of the ways in which organizations today are putting job analysis to work for them ...

... in JOB EVALUATION:
- Setting wage and salary levels
- Appraising performance
- Establishing incentives
- Determining profit sharing

... in RECRUITING AND PLACEMENT:
- Developing job specifications
- Promoting, transferring, and rotating personnel
- Designing tests
- Vocational counseling
- Matching people with jobs
- Placing the handicapped
- Restructuring jobs
- Enriching jobs

... in LABOR AND PERSONNEL RELATIONS:
- Developing performance standards
- Establishing responsibility
- Establishing authority
- Establishing accountability
- Handling grievances
- Conducting labor negotiations
- Establishing communication channels
- Organizing personnel records

... in UTILIZATION OF WORKERS:
- Organizing and planning
- Engineering jobs
- Controlling costs
- Predicting changes
- Avoiding task duplication

... in TRAINING:
- Developing training courses
- Selecting trainees
- Orienting new workers
- Programming teaching machines

If your job analysis program has been in operation for some time, you can probably add a few uses of your own here. The point is that the time and expense involved in conducting a periodic job analysis is well justified, in most cases. Programs that *aren't* bringing an adequate return on the investment are probably suffering from (among other things) a lack of corporate imagination. It is suggested that no matter what the status of your current program—from nonexistent to well-established—you set "better utilization of job information" as one of your primary goals for the future.

One way of determining how much "mileage" you are getting out of an existing job analysis program is to survey managers and supervisors to find out how they are using the information received. Such a survey can be conducted fairly simply with a questionnaire similar to that on the following page. The results can then be collated and you'll have a clear picture of where your program now stands. Don't be surprised if you discover that job analysis information is being utilized primarily for job evaluation and the setting of wage and salary levels, with perhaps limited use as a recruitment and selection aid. This is the case in the majority of organizations today, but it is a situation that can usually be remedied by a combination of improved job analysis practices and a little "consciousness-raising" among company managers. By focusing their attention on the limitations they are imposing on the program, and by educating them on the benefits to be realized through more extensive use of job information, you are providing a valuable service to management and employees alike.

JOB ANALYSIS PROGRAM SURVEY

1. Describe briefly the extent of your participation in the job analysis program.

2. What do you consider the primary purpose of conducting a periodic job analysis?

3. Place an "x" in the box opposite each of the areas listed below in which you utilize the information gathered during job analysis on a *regular, continuing* basis.

Recruiting	☐	Establishing responsibility, authority, accountability	☐
Selection	☐	Resolving conflicts, handling grievances	☐
Placement	☐	Labor relations	☐
Orientation	☐	Personnel records	☐
Job evaluation	☐	Accounting and budget control	☐
Performance appraisal	☐	Training	☐
Safety & health	☐	Other uses:	
EEO planning and analysis	☐	_____	☐
Manpower planning	☐	_____	☐

4. In what areas do you think job information could be put to better use? How?

5. By what method(s) is job information currently being collected in your department?

6. Do you think this technique is effective?

7. What other data-gathering methods would you like to see employed? Why?

A "Job Analysis Program Survey" like the sample above does more than reveal how job information is currently being used. It also asks for some managerial input on how the program could be improved. You might want to expand this questionnaire by adding some questions of your own.

Unfortunately, most companies who survey their existing job analysis programs are disappointed by their findings. In many cases the participation of supervisors and managers in the program is very limited, and most of them cannot even answer questions about data-gathering techniques, etc., because they either don't know or don't care. A program that lacks broad-based participation and support warrants a thorough reevaluation from start to finish. It may be that new techniques must be developed, or that job analysts need further training. Because the steps involved in revamping an unsuccessful program and instituting a new one are basically the same, we will proceed now to look at them in detail.

Preparing For Job Analysis 4

The first step in a job analysis study is for the analyst to become as familiar as possible with the jobs to be analyzed. Even if the analyst has been a member of the personnel department or has worked in the company for several years, it is suggested that he or she review as much material as possible about the jobs and the characteristics of the industry. Information for this purpose may be obtained from the following sources:
1. Books, periodicals and other literature on technical subjects relevant to the jobs that have been selected for analysis.
2. Flow charts, organizational charts, and job descriptions that have been prepared for the organization in the past.
3. Technical literature on industrial processes and job descriptions prepared by trade associations, trade unions, and professional societies.
4. Pamphlets, books, and job descriptions prepared by Federal, state, and municipal government agencies which have an interest in the industry or occupational area; for example, the publications of the U.S. Dept. of Labor, the Occupational Safety and Health Administration, etc.

Many job analysts undertaking such studies for the first time may be familiar with the company's structure and the content of the jobs to be analyzed, but only in a very superficial way. A primary goal of the preparation stage is to expand this knowledge as far as is possible without actually observing the jobs and talking to the incumbents. This will come later.

Another goal of the preparation stage is to make decisions about specific aspects of the program. For example, the analyst must come up with answers to

the following:
- (1) What kind of information will be collected?
- (2) How will this information be obtained and presented?
- (3) What data-gathering method will be used?
- (4) Who will be the "agent" through which this information is obtained (the job analyst, the supervisor, the jobholder, etc.)?

Possible answers to each of these questions are discussed below.

WHAT KIND OF INFORMATION WILL BE COLLECTED?

Much of this has already been covered in our earlier discussion of "What Is Analyzed?" But let's review some of the types of information that can be obtained through job analysis:

- **Job-oriented activities,** including what the jobholder does (inspecting, cleaning, welding, etc.) and in some cases *how, why,* and *when* specific activities are performed.
- **Employee-oriented activities,** including human behaviors (communicating, resolving conflicts, etc.) and job demands (energy expended, etc.).
- **Work procedures,** including specific processes, records that must be maintained, and individual responsibility or accountability.
- **Performance standards,** including how work is measured, the standards that must be met, and the consequences of errors.
- **Equipment, tools, and work aids,** including the machines used, the items or materials worked on, the products made or services delivered, and the area of knowledge dealt with (physics, law, etc.).
- **Job environment,** including working conditions, physical or emotional stress, incentives, social contacts, job-oriented contacts, etc.
- **Job requirements,** including education, experience, skills, etc., required to perform the job successfully, and personal attributes (personality traits, special aptitudes, etc.).

Your own list may be even more extensive, depending upon the uses of the information obtained. For example, if you plan to use job analysis as a means of determining training needs and developing training programs, you'll want to obtain even more in-depth information on "performance standards" and "job requirements."

HOW WILL THIS INFORMATION BE OBTAINED AND PRESENTED?

This refers to the various job analysis techniques—observation, interviews, questionnaires, diary/log, etc.—that will be dealt with later in the section. Most of these methods have some special advantages (or disadvantages) in terms of the type, form, or adequacy of the information that can be elicited, the amount of time they require, the personnel that must be involved, and so forth. But the decision can't really be made until all of the available alternatives have been thoroughly explored.

Job information can be stated in qualitative or quantitative terms, or a combination of both. A qualitative presentation might be a narrative description of job content, working conditions, interpersonal contacts, and personnel requirements. A quantitative presentation, on the other hand, would be based on "units" of information; for example, a listing of job tasks, or statements concerning production per unit of time.

If job analysis is being performed primarily to produce updated job descriptions, the information collected may be translated almost directly into the established job description format. But this can limit the usefulness of the information by putting it in a form that is not only rigidly structured but that may have a "reputation" for limited access. In most cases the information collected during job analysis will be far more comprehensive than that used in the preparation of a one or two-page job description. It should therefore be maintained in separate form so that it can be put to other specialized uses.

WHO WILL BE THE "AGENT" THROUGH WHICH THIS INFORMATION IS OBTAINED?

In most cases this will be an individual—the job analyst, the supervisor, the incumbent—or a combination of two or more individuals. But occasionally a device of some sort is used (for example, a camera) to record job information. In any case, the extent of employee and supervisory participation will have to be determined, and the role of the job analyst will have to be set forth in some detail before any organized attempt at analyzing jobs can be made.

DETERMINING YOUR PROGRAM OBJECTIVES

Another step in preparing for job analysis is to determine your program objectives. If a job analysis program of some sort has been in operation at your firm for a number of years, the original objectives may have been long forgotten or rendered obsolete. If the program is the first of its kind, then you will naturally want to pinpoint your objectives early on, and design the program with these end results in mind.

It may be helpful to refer back to the list of possible uses of job analysis information to make sure that you are not overlooking an important organizational need. Top management may already have decided on one or two objectives of its own, but this is no reason to ignore other potential uses. It should be recognized, however, that there are limits to the purposes that can reasonably be fulfilled by any given program. Try to decide on a few, and focus your program on achieving them. If you spread the job analysis effort too thin, trying to make it serve a number of different purposes in areas of the company, it may well end up serving none of them adequately.

The important thing is that your objectives should be agreed upon by management, the job analyst, and any personnel specialists who will be involved in the program. It may also be wise to share these objectives with employees when you orient them to the program. If they know ahead of time, for example, that job analysis is being performed in order to eliminate pay inequities or determine training needs, they may be much more willing to cooperate with the job analyst when the time comes.

DEVELOPING JOB ANALYSIS MATERIALS

Once the objectives of your program have been crystallized, the next step is to design or develop the various materials that will be required. The most important of these materials, of course, is the actual form on which job data will be recorded. The particular form design will depend upon the analysis technique (observation, interview, questionnaire, etc.) that you have selected. Samples of appropriate data-gathering forms will be given later when specific analysis techniques are discussed.

No matter what technique you utilize to analyze jobs in your organization, there are certain basic areas of information that will have to be covered. The "Checklist for Job Analysis Forms Design" on the following page will help you evaluate the forms you are now using or design new ones from scratch. Use it to make sure you are not leaving out a vital area of information or including areas that aren't really relevant. See also the "Job Analysis Schedule" used by the federal government to record job analysis data. This schedule is printed later in this volume.

CHECKLIST FOR JOB ANALYSIS FORMS DESIGN

[Instructions: Use this checklist to evaluate existing data-gathering forms or to design a new one. Your form should ask appropriate questions in each of the eight areas listed below. The subheadings under each area suggest specific questions that might be asked.]

- ☐ 1. **JOB IDENTITY**
    - ☐ Job title
    - ☐ Department
    - ☐ Location or facility
    - ☐ Number of incumbents
- ☐ 2. **WORK PERFORMED**
    - ☐ What duties/responsibilities are performed
    - ☐ How they are performed
    - ☐ Why they are performed
    - ☐ Frequency and scope of specific duties
- ☐ 3. **KNOWLEDGE REQUIRED**
    - ☐ Areas of knowledge
    - ☐ General disciplines
    - ☐ Specialized expertise
    - ☐ Formal education (how much)
    - ☐ Experience (how long)
- ☐ 4. **SKILLS REQUIRED**
    - ☐ Mental (computational, analytical, abstract, etc.)
    - ☐ Physical (visual, dexterity, etc.)
    - ☐ Interpersonal (selling, counseling, supervising, etc.)
- ☐ 5. **PHYSICAL DEMANDS**
    - ☐ Exertion; availability of support equipment
    - ☐ Motion
    - ☐ Environment; heat, cold, humidity, noise
    - ☐ Hazards
    - ☐ Exposure to unpleasant conditions
- ☐ 6. **SPECIAL DEMANDS**
    - ☐ Work hours
    - ☐ Travel
    - ☐ Isolation

☐ 7. **SOURCES OF WORKERS FOR THIS JOB:**
    ☐ From other jobs (identify)
    ☐ Job posting
    ☐ Apprenticeship programs (how long)
    ☐ Other companies; what type of work
    ☐ Hands-on training

☐ 8. **ACCOUNTABILITY**
    ☐ Equipment value
    ☐ Assets
    ☐ Budgets and expenditures
    ☐ Outside relations

Another essential item for job analysis is an up-to-date organizational chart. It can tell you at a glance the existing relationships and lines of authority among various jobs, help you identify "benchmark jobs" (the key jobs in the organization that are selected first for analysis), and can alert you to jobs that are out-of-line and may need to be restructured or relocated within the organizational hierarchy. A separate organizational chart should be prepared for top management and for each department in which jobs are to be analyzed. While this may sound like an overwhelming task, the time and confusion it can save in the long run make it well worthwhile. Such charts can usually be prepared (if they do not already exist) quite easily with the help of personnel staff members and department heads. Department or division heads can even prepare charts for their own areas, and a personnel staffer can then coordinate the multiple charts into a companywide one. Some sample charts appear on the pages that follow.

Another approach is to prepare an organizational outline. This is similar to an organizational chart, but it is not presented graphically. As the name suggests, it is an outline of the company's (or department's) general structure and reporting relationships. For example, the organizational outline for the employee relations department of a manufacturing plant might look something like this:

1. Plant General Manager
   1.1 Product Line I Manager
   1.2 Product Line II Manager
   1.3 Product Line III Manager
   1.4 Product Line IV Manager
   1.5 Employee Relations Manager
      1.5.1 Staff Assistant
      1.5.2 Recruiting and Staffing Manager
          1.5.2.1 Exempt Recruiting Specialist
          1.5.2.2 Nonexempt Recruiting Specialist
          1.5.2.3 Nonexempt Interviewer
      1.5.3 Plant Safety Coordinator
      1.5.4 Employee Benefits Administrator
      1.5.5 Wage and Salary Administrator
          1.5.5.1 Job Analyst
          1.5.5.2 Personnel Records Supervisor

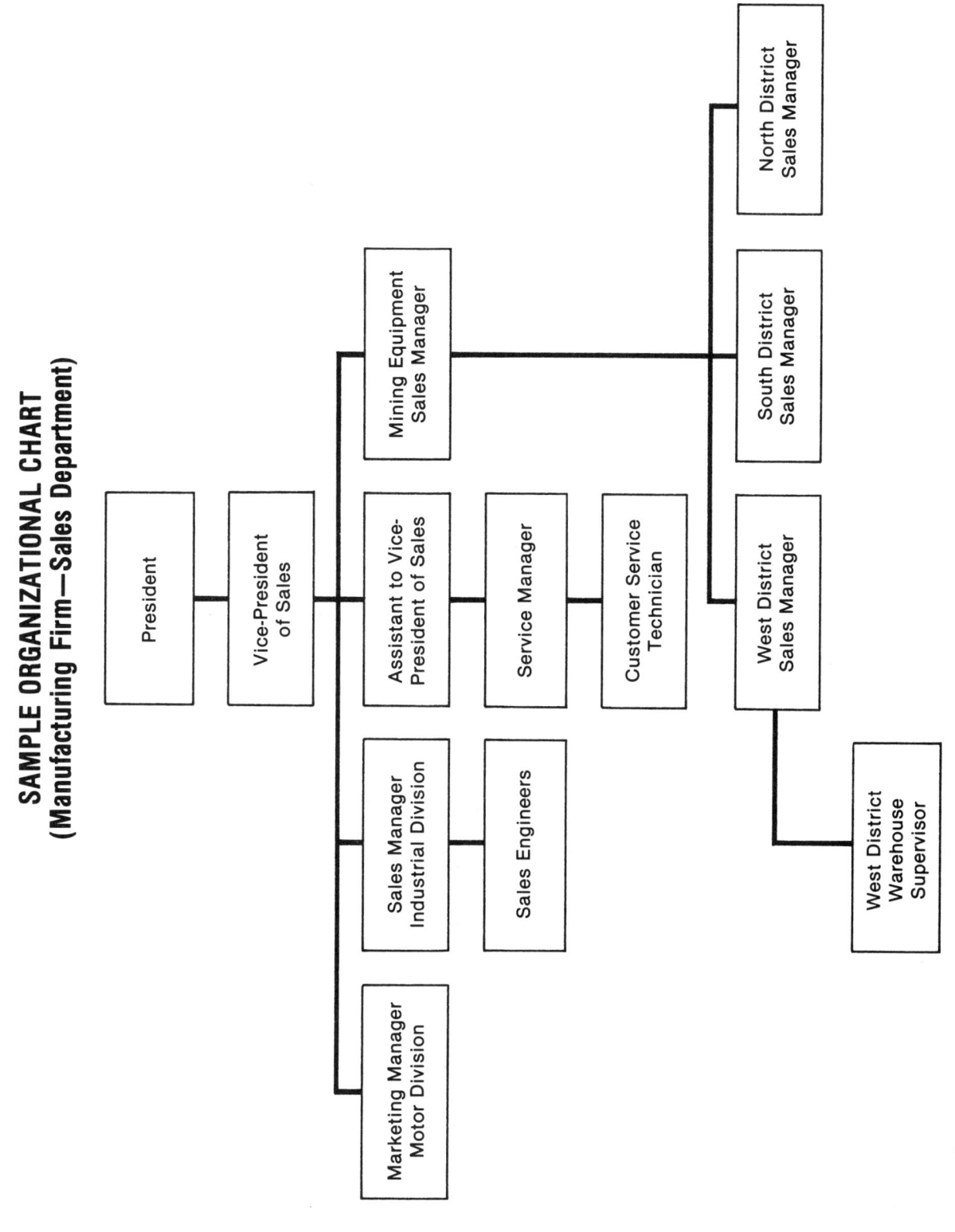

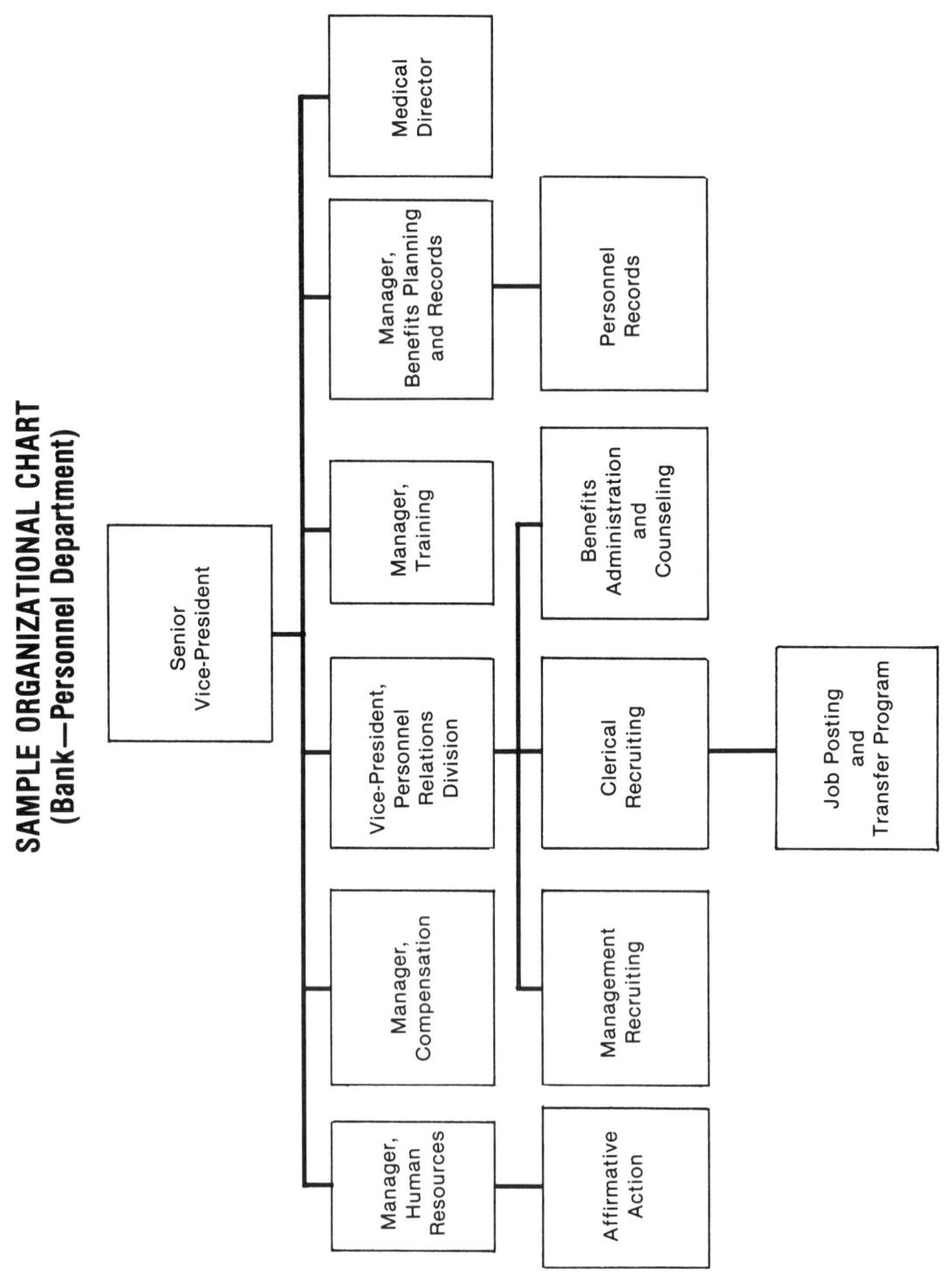

SAMPLE ORGANIZATIONAL CHART
(Bank—Personnel Department)

Whether you decide to represent your organization's framework diagrammatically or in outline form, the idea is to keep it as simple and easy-to-read as possible, showing only job titles and lines of authority. Job analysis may eventually reveal that the *real* working relationships do not correspond in all cases to those shown on the organizational chart. The chart can then be redrawn to reflect the changes that have evolved on their own or that were a direct result of the job analysis program.

IDENTIFYING BENCHMARK JOBS

Organizational charts do more than just give the analyst a good overall view of the company. They can be very helpful in the process of identifying what are called "benchmark jobs." These are the jobs within the organization that are selected to be analyzed first. While the term is usually used in the context of job evaluation or comparative wage surveys, benchmark jobs serve an important purpose in job analysis as well. The job analyst facing his task for the first time might be tempted to start at the top of the organizational hierarchy and work down—or vice versa. But there is a good possibility with either approach that he will run into snags before long. The advantage in starting out with benchmark jobs is that they are fairly well defined and understood to begin with, and they provide the analyst with a reference point from which he can move more easily to less well defined, less easily understood jobs.

How do you know which jobs in your company should be considered "benchmark" jobs? The basic criteria are as follows:

(1) The job should be immediately recognizable, so that the individuals who are asked to provide job information will not be confused about the job being analyzed.
(2) The job should have a relatively large number of incumbents.
(3) The job should be one that remains relatively unchanged, so that it will provide a stable basis for analysis and for comparison with other jobs.
(4) The job should be a good reference point as far as level and responsibility are concerned. In other words, benchmark jobs should be selected at low, intermediate, and high levels in major areas throughout the company.

In summary, benchmark jobs are those that can be precisely defined, with titles that are not easily misconstrued. They are also performed in a more or less similar manner by most organizations. They have approximately the same content and skill requirements wherever they are found. Examples of benchmark jobs would be "tool and die maker," "electrician," and "janitor."

SELECTING AND TRAINING THE JOB ANALYST

We've already talked a little about the qualifications of a good job analyst. But if the analyst is selected from within the ranks of the personnel department, he or she will need training and coaching before the actual job analysis program can be put into operation. Ideally, the analyst should be selected several months in advance, so that he has adequate time to prepare for his role. If a professional job analyst is brought in from outside, he will still need some time to get acquainted with the company's procedures and organization.

No matter where analysts come from, they should receive thorough training in the company's job evaluation plan and any other existing programs that are closely linked to job analysis and the writing of job descriptions. If a union is involved, the training period should include a close study of relevant portions of the union contract. Above all, however, newly selected analysts should be thoroughly familiar with company policies and the organizational structure, so that they know what departments do what, at what level certain types of conflict are resolved, etc. The final stage of training usually includes accompanying experienced analysts as they make a job study. The next job study might be performed by the new analyst, with the experienced individual observing and providing guidance along the way.

Even after the new analyst is judged capable of performing on her own, her work should be reviewed closely for several months to insure that it is consistent with what has been done before. Because the many different skills involved in job analysis can only be mastered through experience, it is obvious that the training and learning process will take a considerable amount of time, and that the newly selected analyst should not be expected to launch a new program or continue an existing one until this learning stage has been completed.

INTRODUCING THE PROGRAM TO PARTICIPANTS

Most employees and even managers who have not been involved in a job analysis program before have no idea what job analysis is or what it is meant to achieve. If the job analyst suddenly appears at the work site and starts asking questions and taking notes, the natural reaction is going to be resentment and suspicion (if not open hostility) and an unwillingness to cooperate. This is why it is so important to introduce the program properly to all those who may be affected or asked to participate.

There are three basic areas in which employees should be informed: (1) the goals of the analysis program; (2) who will be involved; and (3) exactly what is going to happen. A wide variety of media are available to communicate information in these areas: small group meetings, bulletin boards, company newspapers, or special memos. Let's say that the program is being conducted primarily for wage and salary administration purposes. A sample introductory memo to employees might look something like this:

To: All Employees
From: Robert Meier, Company President

XYZ Inc. recognizes the fact that each one of you is interested in the company's pay policies and the procedures used in determining wage and salary levels. In our effort to develop a compensation program that is fair and acceptable to all concerned, we have established the following objectives:
(1) Each of you must understand the duties and responsibilities that comprise your job; there should be no discrepancies between your understanding and management's understanding of what the job entails;
(2) Each of you should be rewarded fairly and equitably on the basis of the skills, knowledge and ability you bring to your job.

To achieve these objectives, we are conducting job analyses. If your job is one of those selected for analysis, you will receive detailed information on your role. Whether or not your job is analyzed, you can make a valuable contribution to the success of this program by giving the job analyst your full cooperation.

Thank you.

A follow-up memo can then be sent to those employees whose jobs are selected for analysis. Here is a sample:

TO: Employees whose jobs have been selected for job analysis
FROM: Helen Morrissey, Vice-President/Personnel

As your supervisor has already notified you, your job has been selected for detailed analysis by Sam Black, our newly appointed job analyst. We chose your job because it is representative of many other similar jobs, *not* because *you* perform it. In other words, it has nothing to do with you as a person or how well you've been performing lately; this is strictly an analysis of the job itself.

Here are a few facts of which you should be aware before the analysis starts:
- Under no circumstances will your pay be cut as a result of the job analysis; in some cases, pay *may* be increased.
- *You* will benefit from the job analysis because it will help you, your supervisor, and management to understand what you are supposed to be doing.
- The job analyst is an objective observer; he is there merely to report on what he observes, not to pass judgment on you or what you say about the job. Therefore, the more open and honest you are with him, the more you'll benefit in the end.

We hope that you'll give Mr. Black your full cooperation. If you have any questions about the job analysis program, please address them either to me or to your immediate supervisor.

It is especially important that there be good rapport between the job analyst and line supervisors—a prime area for unnecessary conflict and misunderstanding. Job analysis sessions often become an emotional battleground, because both individuals approach the job from different points of view and with different objectives in mind. In reality, it is to their mutual advantage to develop the most accurate possible picture of the job. The analyst can help the supervisor by probing for facts and drawing comparisons that are beyond the scope of the supervisor's experience or knowledge. In turn, the line manager can serve as a check on the analyst's judgment.

Most conflicts between analysts and line supervisors arise because personal prejudices and egos get in the way of objective perceptions about the job. Supervisors, for example, may feel that the analyst is "belittling" the jobs that report to them by reducing them to simple lists of tasks and equipment used. Or they may take issue over a particular job simply because they feel threatened by or dislike the incumbent personally. Nor is the job analyst immune to personal foibles. Personality clashes can cause the analyst to approach certain jobs with a less-than-open-minded attitude, and the resulting analyses can actually hurt the incumbents' pay levels or opportunities for advancement.

All of these, of course, are situations to be strictly avoided. Careful selection procedures for job analysts and a thorough orientation effort for line supervisors can go a long way toward heading off such problems. While it is only natural for employees and supervisors alike to feel a little uncomfortable about the job analyst's presence, most of their discomfort and suspicion can be alleviated by having the manager or department head make a point of introducing analysts to employees and taking them on a tour of the area before the actual job study begins.

A Helpful Resource: The Department of Labor's *Handbook for Analyzing Jobs*

If your firm has never undertaken job analysis before, there are a number of helpful resources available. The experiences of other companies in your industry or area are the most obvious source of information, and there are a number of books available through university or business school libraries. But perhaps one of the most accessible resources is the *Handbook for Analyzing Jobs* produced by the U.S. Training and Employment Service. This volume is devoted to an explanation of the procedures and techniques used in the public employment service to obtain and present job analysis information. Although the techniques here were developed with the occupational information needs of the various government manpower programs in mind, many of them can be applied to any job analysis program.

The *Handbook* breaks down job information into two categories, and then

seeks specific information under the following subheadings:
1. **Work performed:**
   Worker functions
   Work fields
      Methods verbs
      Machines, tools, equipment, and work aids
   Materials, products, subject matter, and services
2. **Worker traits:**
   Training time
   Aptitudes
   Temperaments
   Interests
   Physical demands and environmental conditions

The bulk of the *Handbook* is taken up by comprehensive listings of the type of information that might come under each of these subheadings. While this is a highly structured approach to job analysis and it requires a degree of specificity and detail that would simply not be necessary in many companies, it might be worthwhile here to take a brief look at each of the categories of job information listed above and some relevant examples just to get some idea of exactly what kind of data the job analyst is after.

Worker Functions. This category deals with the worker's relationship to data, people, and things. Each function has an identifying number; the lower the identifying number, the higher the level (i.e., complexity) of that particular function. A combination of the highest functions that the worker performs in relation to data, people, and things expresses the total level of complexity of the job.

Work Fields. The *Handbook* lists 100 work fields for the purpose of classifying all the jobs in the economy. Each work field has a title, a definition, and a three-digit identifying number. They range from the specific (drafting, riveting, sawing, etc.) to the general (structural-fabricating-installing-repairing). Although a single job may involve techniques specific to a number of work fields, it should be characterized in terms of its primary involvement. For example, a job of mixing ingredients may also include weighing them. This would be identified by the work field of "mixing," with the work field of "weighing" as a subsidiary. Each work field is followed by a list of methods verbs and its characteristic machines, tools, equipment, and work aids.

Methods Verbs. These are verbs (action words) which are used to denote the specific methods of performing the work. They tell how the objectives of the work field are accomplished and relate to the technology or area of knowledge that is basic to a specific work field. For example, under the work field "Hoisting-Conveying," methods verbs include "digging," "dragging," "dredging," "pulling," "pushing," "scooping," "scraping," and "shoveling."

Some of these verbs occur in more than one work field and their meanings may change accordingly.

Machines, Tools, Equipment, and Work Aids. "Machines" are defined as the devices "designed to apply a force to do work on or move materials or to process data." Examples would be printing presses, drill presses, conveyors, locomotives, automobiles, adding machines, and typewriters. "Tools" are defined as "implements which are manipulated to do work on or move materials." They include hand tools plus those manipulated by the worker through outside power sources (pneumatic hammers, cutting torches, paint-spray guns, etc.). "Equipment" includes devices which generate power, communicate signals, or have an effect upon material through the application of light, heat, electricity, steam, chemicals or atmospheric pressure. Examples are ovens, forges, cameras, and power-generated devices. "Work aids" are miscellaneous items which cannot be considered machines, tools, or equipment and yet are necessary for carrying out the work. They include jigs, fixtures, and clamps; special measuring devices (micrometers, gages, rules, ets.); graphic instructions (blueprints, sketches, instruction manuals, maps, charts, etc.); and musical instruments.

Materials, Products, Subject Matter and Services. These include (1) basic materials being processed, such as wood, fabric, or metal; (2) final products being made, such as automobiles or baskets; (3) data dealt with or applied, such as in insurance or physics; and (4) services, such as barbering or dentistry.

Training Time. This is the amount of general educational development and specific vocational preparation required for a worker to gain the knowledge and abilities necessary for average performance in the job.

Aptitudes. These are the specific capacities or abilities required of an individual in order to facilitate the learning of a task or job duty. They include intelligence; verbal, numerical, and spatial aptitude; motor coordination; manual dexterity; and color discrimination.

Interests. An interest is defined as "a tendency to become absorbed in an experience and to continue it, while an aversion is a tendency to turn away from it to something else." The five interest factors are therefore set up as opposites. An example would be:

A preference for activities of a routine, concrete, organized nature.	vs.	A preference for activities of an abstract and creative nature.

Temperaments. These are defined as "personal traits" required by specific job-worker situations. The *Handbook* lists 10 such temperaments, an example of which would be, "Adaptability to performing repetitive work, or to performing continuously the same work, according to set procedures, sequence or pace."

Physical Demands. These include strength (lifting, carrying, pushing, pulling); climbing or balancing; stooping, kneeling, crouching, and/or crawling;

reaching, handling, fingering, and/or feeling; talking and/or hearing; and seeing.

Environmental Conditions. These are physical surroundings that make specific demands upon a worker's physical capacity. They include work location (inside, outside, or both); extreme heat or cold (with or without temperature changes); wetness and/or humidity; noise and/or vibration; special hazards; and atmospheric conditions.

The *Handbook* discusses only one technique for gathering job data, which it refers to as "observation-interview." It also presents standardized forms for the collection and presentation of job analysis information, an example of which can be seen on the following pages. But for the average employer approaching job analysis for the first time, the *Handbook* is most valuable as a source of appropriate vocabulary and an excellent example of how to break down even the most complex jobs into well-defined component parts. While there may be no point in reading the *Handbook* cover-to-cover, it would be wise at least to study some of the introductory material (there are good sections on how to conduct a job analysis interview, how to design organizational and process flow charts, etc.) and to familiarize yourself with the basic job information areas described above. You can order the *Handbook for Analyzing Jobs* from the Superintendent of Documents, U.S. Government Printing Office, Washington, D.C. 20402.

[Note: This is a sample of the form used by the Handbook *both to structure the analysis and to record the resulting data. You may want to use it in designing a similar form more suited to your company's needs.]*

JOB ANALYSIS SCHEDULE

1. Estab. Job Title DOUGH MIXER
2. Ind. Assign. (bake. prod.)
3. SIC Code(s) and Title(s) 2051 Bread and other bakery products

Code 520.782
WTA Group Oper. Control p. 435
DOT Title
Ind. Desig.

4. JOB SUMMARY:

    Operates mixing machine to mix ingredients for straight and sponge (yeast) doughs according to established formulas, directs other workers in fermentation of dough, and cuts dough into pieces with hand cutter.

5. WORK PERFORMED RATINGS:

    Worker Functions

D Data	P People	(T) Things
5	6	2

    Work Field 146 - Cooking, Food Preparing

    M.P.S.M.S. 384 - Bakery Products

6. WORKER TRAITS RATINGS:

    GED   1 (2) 3 4 5 6

    SVP   1 2 3 (4) 5 6 7 8 9

    Aptitudes G 3 V 3 N 3 S 3 P 3 Q 4 K 3 F 3 M 3 E 4 C 4

    Temperaments D F I J (M) P R S (T) V

    Interests   (1a) 1b 2a 2b 3a 3b 4a (4b) 5a (5b)

    Phys. Demands S L M (H) V 2 (3)(4) 5 (6)

    Environ. Cond. (I) O B 2 3 4 (5) 6 7

MA 7-36

7. General Education

    a. Elementary 6   High School _____ Courses _____

    b. College None Courses _____

8. Vocational Preparation

    a. College None Courses _____

    b. Vocational Education None Courses _____

    c. Apprenticeship None _____

    d. Inplant Training None _____

    e. On-the-Job Training six months _____

    f. Performance on Other Jobs DOUGH-MIXER HELPER --- One year

9. Experience One year as DOUGH-MIXER HELPER

10. Orientation Four hours

11. Licenses, etc. Food Handlers Certificate issued by the Health Department

12. Relation to Other Jobs and Workers

    Promotion: From DOUGH-MIXER HELPER   To BAKER

    Transfers: From None   To None

    Supervision Received By BAKER

    Supervision Given DOUGH-MIXER HELPER

---

13. Machines, Tools, Equipment, and Work Aids — Dough-mixing machine; balance scales; hand scoops; measuring vessels; portable dough troughs.

14. Materials and Products

    Bread dough

15. Description of Tasks:

1. Dumps ingredients into mixing machine: Examines production schedule to determine type of bread to be produced, such as rye, whole wheat, or white. Refers to formula card for quantities and types of ingredients required, such as flour, water, milk, vitamin solutions, and shortening. Weighs out, measures, and dumps ingredients into mixing machine. (20%)

2. Operates mixing machine: Turns valves and other hand controls to set mixing time according to type of dough being mixed. Presses button to start agitator blades in machine. Observes gages and dials on equipment continuously to verify temperature of dough and mixing time. Feels dough for desired consistency. Adds water or flour to mix measuring vessels and adjusts mixing time and controls to obtain desired elasticity in mix. (55%)

3. Directs other workers in fermentation of dough: Prepares fermentation schedule according to type of dough being raised. Sprays portable dough Trough with lubricant to prevent adherence of mixed dough to trough. Directs DOUGH-MIXER HELPER in positioning trough beneath door of mixer to catch dough when mixing cycle is complete. Pushes or directs other workers to push troughs of dough into fermentation room. (10%)

4. Cuts dough: Dumps fermentated dough onto worktable. Manually kneads dough to eliminate gases formed by yeast. Cuts dough into pieces with hand cutter. Places cut dough on proofing rack and covers with cloth. (10%)

5. Performs miscellaneous duties: Records on work sheet number of batches mixed during work shift. Informs BAKE SHOP FOREMAN when repairs or major adjustments are required for machines and equipment. (5%)

16. Definition of Terms

   <u>Trough</u> — A long, narrow, opened vessel used for kneading or washing ingredients.

17. General Comments

   None

18. Analyst Jane Smith   Date 3/21/70   Editor John Rilley   Date 3/30/70
    Reviewed By Alexandra Purcey   Title, Org. Foreman, Bake Shop
    National Office Reviewer Mary Moore

Methods And Techniques 5

There are more than a dozen different approaches to gathering job analysis information that have proved successful. But of these, there are five or six that seem to have established themselves as "traditional"—that is, they have been widely used for many years in a variety of organizations and institutions. While four of these traditional approaches will be discussed in some detail later, we will take a brief look at each of them here:

Observation. Direct observation by a trained analyst while the incumbent is actually engaged in performing job duties is a very common method for obtaining job information. This technique is particularly appropriate for low-level jobs that possess short and largely observable work cycles. Low-skill workers are also likely to find it difficult to put their job duties into words, so observation can sidestep this hurdle.

Videotape and voice recordings of employees as they perform their jobs is a variation on this approach, although it has in some cases raised ethical questions if employees are not informed of the taping. But as a job analysis technique it has been used with success in both the airline and hotel industries.

Interviews. Interviewing is a useful technique for getting information that can't be obtained by observing the employee at work. Interviews can also be used to verify the facts collected by other methods, such as observation or written questionnaires. The job is analyzed through a face-to-face interview with the worker performing the job, his or her superior, or with a group of employees who perform or interact with a specific job. Interviews are usually conducted at the job site, although such factors as noise, weather, safety, privacy, or management preferences may make another site more desirable.

Questionnaires. This is probably the least expensive way of gathering job information. A well-designed questionnaire can also be the most efficient way to collect such information in a relatively short period of time. But many employers feel that questionnaires alone can't do the job and therefore use them to supplement the information gathered by other means. Generally speaking, questionnaires are most successful when used by white-collar, professional, managerial and administrative employees.

Diary/Log. This method represents a less structured approach than the written questionnaire. The employee is asked to record his daily tasks and activities in a log or self-reporting diary. This enables the job analyst to gather information not only on the tasks performed but on the percentage of time spent on each. However, it requires considerable diligence on the employee's part, and many workers simply lack the skill and discipline to record their activities in clear, concise language.

Panel of Experts. Useful information about a job can often be gathered by getting together with other employees working in the area, employees or supervisors from other companies performing similar jobs, and in-house "experts" on the job being studied. This technique is very useful in an unstable environment, where job analysis must be performed on newly created jobs.

Combination Approach. Almost any combination of the above described methods will achieve better results than a single method used alone. The observation-interview method (recommended by the *Handbook for Analyzing Jobs*) is probably the best combination in most cases for gathering and recording job information. In fact, observation can be used successfully with any of the other methods; five or ten minutes of direct on-site observation can often reveal more than pages of questionnaire responses.

No matter what job analysis technique is used, answers to the same basic questions must be obtained (e.g., what are the job duties and responsibilities? education, experience and skill requirements? basic accountabilities? environmental conditions? mental, emotional and physical demands? health and safety considerations?). And sooner or later, the answers to these questions are going to have to be put in written form. The "Job Analysis Schedule" used by the U.S. Training and Employment Service in its *Handbook for Analyzing Jobs* represents one possible approach to recording job analysis information in a useful written format. Another type of form appears on the next page (see "Job Analysis Information Sheet"). The idea is to get the information *organized* in such a way that it can then be used to write job descriptions or serve whatever other purposes it was designed to serve. A good job information form can be used with any of the six techniques described above.

JOB ANALYSIS INFORMATION SHEET

Job Title _____   Date _____

Job Code _____   Dept. _____

Superior's Title _____ Hours worked ____ am to ____ am
                                                        pm   pm

Job Analyst's Name _____

1. What is the job's overall purpose?

2. If the incumbent supervises others, list them by job title; if there is more than one employee with the same title, put the number in parentheses following.

3. Check those activities that are part of the incumbent's supervisory duties.
   - ☐ Training
   - ☐ Inspecting work
   - ☐ Coaching and/or counseling
   - ☐ Performance Appraisal
   - ☐ Budgeting
   - ☐ Others (please specify)
     _____
     _____

4. Describe the type and extent of supervision received by the incumbent.

5. JOB DUTIES: Describe briefly WHAT the incumbent does and, if possible, HOW he/she does it. Include duties in the following categories:
   a. daily duties (those performed on a regular basis every day or almost every day)

   b. periodic duties (those performed weekly, monthly, quarterly, or at other regular intervals)

   c. duties performed at irregular intervals

6. Is the incumbent performing duties he/she considers unnecessary? If so, describe.

7. Is the incumbent performing duties not presently included in the job description? If so, describe.

8. EDUCATION: Check the box that indicates the educational requirements for the job (*not* the educational background of the incumbent).

- ☐ No formal education required
- ☐ Eighth grade education
- ☐ High school diploma (or equivalent)
- ☐ 2-year college degree (or equivalent)
- ☐ 4-year college degree (or equivalent)
- ☐ graduate work or advanced degree (specify: _____)
- ☐ professional license (specify: _____)

9. EXPERIENCE: Check the amount of experience needed to perform the job.

- ☐ None
- ☐ Less than one month
- ☐ One to six months
- ☐ Six months to one year
- ☐ One to three years
- ☐ Three to five years
- ☐ Five to ten years
- ☐ More than ten years

10. LOCATION: Check location of job and, if necessary or appropriate, describe briefly.

- ☐ Outdoor _____
- ☐ Indoor _____
- ☐ Underground _____
- ☐ Pit _____
- ☐ Scaffold _____
- ☐ Other (specify)

_____

_____

11. ENVIRONMENTAL CONDITIONS: Check any objectionable conditions found on the job and note afterward how frequently each is encountered (rarely, occasionally, constantly, etc.)

- ☐ Dirt _____
- ☐ Dust _____
- ☐ Heat _____
- ☐ Cold _____
- ☐ Noise _____
- ☐ Fumes _____
- ☐ Odors _____
- ☐ Wetness/humidity _____
- ☐ Vibration _____
- ☐ Sudden temperature changes _____
- ☐ Darkness or poor lighting _____
- ☐ Other (specify)

_____

_____

12. HEALTH AND SAFETY: Check any undesirable health and safety conditions under which the incumbent must perform and note how often they are encountered.

    ☐ Elevated workplace _____
    ☐ Mechanical hazards _____
    ☐ Explosives _____
    ☐ Electrical hazards _____
    ☐ Fire hazards _____
    ☐ Radiation _____
    ☐ Other (specify)

    _____

    _____

13. MACHINES, TOOLS, EQUIPMENT, AND WORK AIDS: Describe briefly what machines, tools, equipment or work aids the incumbent works with on a regular basis:

14. Have concrete work standards been established (errors allowed, time taken for a particular task, etc.)? If so, what are they?

15. Are there any personal attributes (special aptitudes, physical characteristics, personality traits, etc.) required by the job?

16. Are there any exceptional problems the incumbent might be expected to encounter in performing the job under normal conditions? If so, describe.

17. Describe the successful completion and/or end results of the job.

18. What is the seriousness of error on this job? Who or what is affected by errors the incumbent makes?

19. To what job would a successful incumbent expect to be promoted?

[Note: This form is obviously slanted toward a manufacturing environment. But it can be adapted quite easily to fit a number of different types of jobs.]

WHICH METHOD IS BEST FOR YOUR COMPANY?

With these and so many other data-gathering techniques to choose from, how can the firm without any previous experience in job analysis decide which method is the most appropriate? There are a number of basic considerations that will influence the choice of a job analysis technique, of which the following are probably the most important:

1) **Location:** Will the physical location of the jobs to be analyzed make it too expensive to employ a particular technique?
2) **Work environment:** Will the job environment (noise, heat, wind, or dangerous conditions) make on-site observation too hazardous? Would a questionnaire or diary/log approach be more appropriate?
3) **Technology:** Does the technical nature of the job make one technique more or less advantageous than others?
4) **Nature of work:** Does the way in which the work is performed make a particular method more appropriate than others? Does the routine or complex nature of the job lend itself to a specific method?
5) **Personal and social considerations:** Does the jobholder's educational or cultural background favor or rule out a certain method? Does the level of social interaction among a number of employees working together on a particular job make it clear that one method will work while others simply won't be as effective?

The answers to these questions should point the way toward a specific technique or combination of techniques. If you have performed job analyses in the past, the experience you have gained will also influence your decision. If the technique you used before was not successful, you should try to pinpoint the reasons why and try to make a better choice this time.

Another important consideration in choosing a technique is the knowledge and qualifications of the job analysts. How well do they understand the basic company structure and specific job functions? How well do they relate to employees? How enthusiastic or aggressive are they? Will they be able to improvise or make changes when the situation warrants it? Will they be able to distinguish between contributions to the job that are unique to the incumbent and those that are required by the job itself? Certain methods are better suited to the inexperienced analyst or one who is unfamiliar with the jobs to be analyzed. On-site observation, for example, requires a certain basic understanding of what is going on before the appropriate job information can be taken down. If the technology of the job is too far beyond the analyst's experience and understanding, then perhaps a questionnaire completed by the incumbent would be a better source of job information.

THE AIR FORCE STUDY COMPARING JOB ANALYSIS METHODS

Very few studies comparing the effectiveness of the various job analysis methods have been performed. But several years ago a man named Rupe and his associates carried out such a study in the United States Air Force. It compared the effectiveness of the following five methods:

- Group Interview
- Individual Interview
- Observation Interview (essentially a combination of the observation and interview approaches, with the "interview" aspect carried out at the work site)
- Technical Conference (what was earlier described as the "Panel of Experts" approach)
- Questionnaire Survey (questionnaires filled out by "representative" job incumbents with the assistance of their supervisors, but without the involvement of a job analyst)

Without going into any great detail on the way in which the study of these five methods was conducted, a brief look at the results might shed some light on the issue for the private employer.

Three types of criteria were used in evaluating the five job analysis methods: (1) the number of job elements reported; (2) the tools, equipment, and materials reported; and (3) the time involved in the analysis process. The second criterion (tools, equipment, and materials) was found not to have much impact, so effectiveness was really judged on the basis of the first and last criteria listed above.

Rupe came up with "scores" for each of the methods as well as for random combinations of the four approaches. His findings can be summarized as follows:

1. Rupe found the individual interview to be the most effective and most dependable method. The time involved was about average for the five methods studied.
2. The technical conference and the observation interview were about equal in terms of providing job information, but they were also the two most expensive methods in terms of time involved.
3. The group interview and questionnaire survey methods were generally found to be the least satisfactory methods. In fact, the group interview was found to be the least effective of the five methods studied, although, in terms of man-hours, it was the least costly of the four methods involving the participation of a job analyst. The questionnaire survey method (which did not utilize an analyst) was obviously the least costly of all.
4. Combining the information derived from two or more methods had a considerable impact on the total amount of information obtained. However, it should be kept in mind that such combinations represent the consolidation of information about positions that may vary widely in

terms of job activities. But this still makes the point that a combination approach can achieve greater coverage of the job in question.

THE IMPORTANCE OF FLEXIBILITY

It can be seen quite clearly from the preceding discussion that there is no single analysis technique that consistently achieves superior results. The type of organization, the background and qualifications of the personnel involved in the program, and the jobs themselves will all have a significant impact on the decision of what approach to utilize. The important thing to remember is that no method comes with a written guarantee. You may get halfway through your first attempt at analyzing jobs and discover that your questionnaire just isn't eliciting the type of information you want, or that employees are too busy with their work to take time off for lengthy personal interviews. The ability to recognize when a particular technique isn't working and to stand back for a moment and survey the alternatives is essential for the job analyst and personnel manager alike. While it may be time-consuming and frustrating to have to abandon the technique you have spent weeks or months developing, imagine the frustration you would feel if you pushed on with the program and ended up with files full of worthless information!

Flexibility is an important ingredient in any job analysis effort. One reason why combination approaches are a good idea is because they have a certain amount of flexibility built in; that is, if one method proves to be less successful, the other can take up the "slack." Don't forget that there are variables beyond your control that must be encountered and dealt with, the human personality being one of them. While the organization of your program, the qualifications of the analyst, and the design of your written forms may be superior, there's always the possibility that employees won't open up or cooperate because they don't understand the program's goals or because they simply don't trust the job analyst. A flexible attitude enables you to take these setbacks in stride and to deal with them in a constructive manner. If further orientation and education about the program are what is called for, then you might even have to stop job analysis in midstream to deal with employees' anxieties and to squelch the rumors that may be damaging their morale.

Obviously you'll want to do everything in your power to choose the right technique from the start. This involves a careful study of not only traditional but some of the more innovative job analysis methods now in operation. We will examine the four basic methods—observation, interviews, questionnaires, and diary/log—below in some detail before moving on to look at some of the newer approaches.

OBSERVATION

Observation as a job analysis technique is the gathering of information by actually watching workers perform their daily tasks. It is most widely used in the factory or for clerical jobs that are fairly repetitious and require relatively little skill. As mentioned earlier, it is most appropriate where the work cycle is brief and the analyst can observe the entire job in a relatively short period of time. If some elements of the job cycle occur at infrequent or irregular intervals, observation may simply not be practical. For example, managerial and administrative jobs are not well suited to this approach.

The major advantage of observation is that information is gathered firsthand, thus eliminating oversights and providing the analyst with a thorough understanding of the job—including working conditions, skills required, equipment used, complexity of the job, and contacts with others. Disadvantages include the time involved, the copious notes that must be taken in order to develop a complete picture of the job, and the employee's reaction to "being watched." There is a tendency for most people to adjust their behavior when they know they are being observed, which then affects the accuracy of the information obtained.

The steps involved in preparing for and carrying out an observation can be summarized as follows:

1. **Introduce the idea to the people who will be involved.** The beginning point for any procedure requiring personal contact is to gain the cooperation of the people involved and to alleviate any worries or suspicions. The purpose of the study should be reviewed with supervisory personnel so they have an understanding of what information is needed and why. A departmental meeting can then be held to communicate this to employees as well.

2. **Get an overall picture of the job(s) under study.** The analyst should study any available written materials pertaining to the jobs that are to be analyzed and talk with the appropriate supervisors or department heads to gain a general knowledge of the work flow, reporting relationships, and other vital aspects of the operations in question.

3. **Select appropriate observation points.** The supervisor should be able to help the analyst select vantage points from which to observe the work. Such posts should be as unobtrusive as possible and yet still permit a clear view of the work as it is being performed. If observation is to be conducted from a number of posts, their sequence should follow the flow of work.

4. **Observe.** The actual observation begins at the work station. The analyst studies the employee as he or she performs the job and tries to determine its overall nature and purpose. Continued observations are then made throughout the course of the work cycle. The analyst tries to organize the pattern of work into a logical sequence, focusing on the most important tasks to get a better idea of the skills, knowledge and abilities required.

5. **Review notes.** Immediately after the observation has been concluded, the analyst sits down and reviews his notes, filling in or expanding on certain items while the information is still "fresh." If further elaboration on some points is required, these items should be noted for later discussion with the employee and the supervisor.

These steps are generally sufficient for hourly rated or relatively routine clerical jobs. But for more complex jobs, the observation technique must usually be replaced or supplemented by personal interviews.

INTERVIEWS

Interviewing in this context is defined as the process of obtaining information for job analysis by questioning the people most directly involved with the job. While it is conceivable that the interviewer and the analyst might be different people, in most cases the same individual performs both functions.

Although the specific requirements for interviewers will vary from company to company, there are certain qualifications that all analyst-interviewers must share. They include the following:

- **Communication skills:** The ability to speak and write well, and to understand what the employee is saying is essential. While it is only natural for most employees to regard the interviewer as an "outsider" to some degree, they will be more likely to open up to someone who shares their job vocabulary and shows that he is able to discuss job content intelligently.

- **Knowledge of jobs in the industry:** The interviewer must possess considerable knowledge of the industry and of the jobs selected for analysis. In fact, he must be acquainted with jobs in general so he can compare and contrast the job under study with other positions in the firm and in the industry as a whole.

- **Judgment and analytical ability:** The interview process requires both good judgment and analytical thinking. The interviewer must not only be able to comprehend what the employee is saying, but to probe for additional facts and to weed out subjective or extraneous information.

- **Objectivity:** There is no room in job analysis interviewing for preconceived ideas, personal biases, or extreme opinions. The individual who can approach the job critically and form independent judgments without being swayed by others is the most likely to succeed as an interviewer.

- **Understanding of human behavior:** An activity that calls for human interaction naturally requires an understanding of personality and behavior. The success of this interaction—and the interview as a whole—depend heavily on the interviewer's ability to motivate the employee to respond openly and honestly. The interviewer must therefore develop rapport and encourage cooperation while at the same time minimizing suspicion, hostility, or embarrassment.

Other favorable personality traits for interviewers include sincerity, integrity and the ability to get along with all types of people. This last quality is perhaps the most important of all, because it is essential that the job analyst be able to develop a good rapport not only with employees but with all levels of management and with other personnel in the job analysis program. The interviewer who is unable to obtain accurate job information, who triggers hostility or suspicion, or who makes a poor impression on employees undermines the entire job analysis effort and can contribute to far more serious employee relations problems in the long run.

PREPARING FOR THE INTERVIEW

The point has already been made that the interviewer must possess considerable knowledge about the industry, the company, and the jobs to be analyzed. The preparation stage should therefore include a study of technical literature pertaining to the industry, company publications (including annual reports), product literature, advertising materials, instruction manuals, previous job analyses, organizational charts, and any other available information that might shed light on the work that is being performed. Job information may also be obtained from existing job descriptions, either those prepared for jobs within the company or for similar positions in other companies. But the analyst should be cautious about relying too heavily on job descriptions that may be out of date or that may introduce biases which could interfere with the gathering of objective information.

A second step in preparing for the interview is to gain the cooperation of the appropriate supervisors and managers. This involves securing the proper authorization for the study and informing supervisory personnel in advance that the interviews are being scheduled. A brief meeting during which the purposes and objectives of the study and the procedures to be followed are reviewed with these individuals can be a good way of enlisting their cooperation in the venture.

The questions to be asked should also be thought out in advance. An interview that has little or no continuity, and during which the analyst must search for the right questions to ask, is likely to elicit incomplete and perhaps even inaccurate or damaging information. The interviewer who is well prepared with questions that have been carefully thought out and organized ahead of time has a much better chance of obtaining the right kind of information from the respondent.

Because the observation and interview techniques are so frequently combined, a tour of the department or on-site inspection of the operations under study is often considered a necessary step in the preparation stage. Whether or not a formal observation is going to be conducted, an informal inspection tour can be valuable. The analyst may be able to notice things about the job that would not ordinarily come up for discussion in the course of the interview.

THE RIGHT SETTING

It is almost impossible to draw any generalizations about the proper setting for a job analysis interview. In some cases it might be desirable to gather the information right at the work site, where the employee can demonstrate certain tasks, show the analyst what files or records are kept, and explain the operation of equipment or machines. On the other hand, on-site interviews mean distractions and little or no privacy. Because the interview is so important to the collection of accurate job information, it deserves the undivided attention of interviewer and employee alike. Unless interruptions are necessary, therefore, it is usually wise to conduct the interview in a place where distractions can be avoided and where privacy is sufficient to allow an honest interchange. Sometimes the best solution is to combine an on-site visit with a private interview.

For managerial and administrative jobs, of course, on-site inspections would have little value. But whatever the job, the office or room used for interviews should be comfortable enough to put the employee at ease. Telephone calls and other interruptions should be prohibited or at least kept to a minimum.

THE INTERVIEW PROCESS

There are three basic principles that should guide any job analysis interview:

(1) The interviewer should always take the initiative. This doesn't mean, however, that the interviewer should dominate the discussion or make the respondent feel defensive.
(2) The interviewer's manner and approach should reflect a sincere interest in what the respondent has to say.
(3) The interviewer should direct the interview toward obtaining the necessary information.

This sounds easier that it often *is*. But like any other job analysis technique, interviewing requires a great deal of practice. Here are some suggestions from the *Handbook for Analyzing Jobs* for getting the interview off to a good start and keeping it on track:

OPENING THE INTERVIEW:

1. Put the worker at ease by learning his name in advance, introducing yourself, and discussing general and pleasant topics long enough to establish rapport.
2. Make the purpose of the interview clear by explaining why it was scheduled, what is expected to be accomplished, and how the worker's cooperation will help in the production of occupational analysis tools used for placement and counseling. Assure him that the interview is not concerned with time study or wages (unless, of course, it is part of a larger job evaluation effort that may indeed result in a new wage and salary structure).
3. Encourage workers to talk by being courteous and showing a sincere interest in what they say.

STEERING THE INTERVIEW:
1. Help the worker to think and talk according to the logical sequence of the duties performed. If duties are not performed in a regular order, ask the worker to describe the duties in a functional manner by taking the most important activity first, the second most important next, and so forth. Request workers to describe the infrequent duties of their jobs, ones that are not part of their regular activities, such as the occasional setup of a machine, occasional repairs, or infrequent reports. Infrequently performed duties, however, do not include periodic or emergency activities such as an annual inventory or the emergency unloading of a freight car.
2. Allow workers sufficient time to answer each question and to formulate an answer. They should be asked only one question at a time.
3. Phrase questions carefully, so that the answers will be more than "yes" or "no."
4. Avoid leading questions (i.e., those with "built-in" answers).
5. Secure specific and complete information pertaining to the two categories of information required for a complete analysis of a job ("work performed" and "worker traits").
6. Conduct the interview in plain, easily understood language.
7. Consider the relationship of the job under analysis to other jobs in the department.
8. Control the interview with respect to the economic use of time and adherence to subject matter. For example, when the interviewee strays from the subject, a good technique for bringing him back to the point is to summarize the data collected up to that point.
9. The interview should be conducted patiently and with consideration for any nervousness or lack of ease on the part of the worker.

CLOSING THE INTERVIEW:
1. Summarize the information obtained from the worker, indicating the major duties performed and the details concerning each of these duties.
2. Close the interview on a friendly note.

MISCELLANEOUS DO'S AND DON'TS FOR INTERVIEWS:
1. Do not take issue with the worker's statements.
2. Do not show any partiality to grievances or conflicts concerning employer-employee relations.
3. Do not show any interest in the wage classification of the job.
4. Be polite and courteous throughout the interview.
5. Do not "talk down" to the worker.

6. Do not permit yourself to be influenced by your personal likes and dislikes.
7. Be impersonal. Do not be critical or attempt to suggest any changes or improvements in organization or methods of work.
8. Talk to workers only with the permission of their supervisors.
9. Verify job data, especially technical or trade terminology, with the supervisor or department head.
10. Verify the completed analysis with the proper official.

The analyst-interviewer must also develop a certain skill in combining note-taking with the conversational aspect of the interview; that is, he or she must be able to take down pertinent facts about the job while maintaining the "flow" of the interview, or to intersperse writing with questions and comments. Some employees will stop talking when they see that the analyst is still busy writing down what they have said. The interviewer should make it clear whether or not she wishes the conversation to continue under these circumstances. Some analysts feel that note-taking inhibits employees from speaking openly and prefer to use a tape recorder or even to record the data from memory immediately after the interview is over. But the latter technique is risky when the job involves a number of complex operations.

PROS AND CONS OF THE INTERVIEW METHOD

The biggest advantage of gathering job analysis information through interviews is that direct person-to-person contact usually provides the analyst with a better understanding of the job. The interview can also be conducted in a more relaxed atmosphere, where the employees don't feel they are being "spied on" and where distractions can be kept to a minimum. If interviews are conducted both with the incumbent and the supervisor, the analyst obtains a comprehensive view of what the job entails.

There are, however, a few drawbacks to this technique. First, there is the possibility that the employee will just clam up. Some people don't respond well in an interview environment; they feel they are being put on the spot and it makes them nervous and uncomfortable. A closely related danger is that the employee may knowingly or unknowingly give inaccurate information about the job, or make statements that she feels obligated to make, even though she knows they are not entirely true. The skilled interviewer, of course, should be able to distinguish facts from inaccurate statements, and will verify important points either through his manner of questioning or by follow-up interviews with supervisors or other incumbents. But the interview as an information-gathering technique is not infallible.

Another problem that frequently accompanies job analysis interviews is that both the employee and the supervisor (assuming that both are interviewed) may end up talking more about the qualifications of the incumbent than about the job content. It may be almost impossible for some workers to separate the qualifications for the job and their own personal qualifications, especially if they think they are performing the job successfully. If the incumbent has been in the position for a long time, it may be equally difficult for his supervisor to draw the distinction. Again, it is up to the job analyst to steer the interview toward a discussion of the job itself, not of how well qualified the incumbent is or how well he or she is performing the job.

INTERVIEW FORMS

Most firms that use the interview technique on a regular basis for job analysis have written forms that not only help the analyst present his questions in a logical order but that also provide a means for organizing the information received. Such forms vary widely, and one company may have several different interview forms for different types of jobs. The sample forms on the pages that follow are representative of a number of different approaches, any of which can easily be adapted to meet your company's job analysis needs.

SAMPLE INTERVIEW FORM
(Clerical, Supervisory and Administrative Positions)

Type of Job: ☐ Clerical
              ☐ Administration
              ☐ Supervisory

Incumbent's Name: _____ **Job Title:**_____

Interviewer's Name:_____

1. Describe in detail the primary or most important duties that you perform daily. If important duties are performed at less frequent intervals, describe them and give the frequency of performance.

2. Describe the secondary duties that you perform at periodic intervals (weekly, monthly, quarterly, etc.) and state the frequency of performance. Also describe any duties you *may* perform.

3. Describe the equipment and/or machines that you use regularly on the job.

4. Describe the working conditions.

5. Describe the proximity, extent, and closeness of any supervision you receive. To what degree does your immediate supervisor outline the methods to be followed, results to be accomplished, check work progress, handle exceptional cases, and check job performance?

6. Describe the kind of supervision you give to other employees. What is the degree of accountability for results in terms of methods, work accomplished, and personnel?

7. How many employees do you supervise directly?_____ indirectly?_____

8. What is the seriousness of error on this job? Who would discover it? Do errors affect your work, the work of others in the department, or persons outside the organization?

9. Are you responsible for any confidential data? State the type of confidential data handled (personnel files, salary information, business secrets, etc.).

10. Are you responsible for money or things of monetary value? State the type of responsibility and the approximate amount you must safeguard.

11. Describe the kind of personal contacts you make (contacts with others in the department, with individuals elsewhere in the company or outside the organization). Can you describe the importance of these contacts to the company?

12. Describe the complexity of your job. What is the degree of independent action you are allowed to take? What decisions are you permitted to make?

13. Describe the type and amount of dexterity or motor skill required. Indicate which job duties require dexterity.

14. Describe the degree of repetitive detail the job involves. Are you frequently bored on the job?

15. List any unusual physical requirements for this job (vision, strength, etc.).

16. What do you feel is necessary in terms of formal education or its equivalent to perform this job satisfactorily?

17. Can you specify the training time needed to arrive at a level of competence on the job?

18. How much job experience (in terms of weeks, months, or years) is needed to perform the job satisfactorily? Where can this type of experience be obtained (inside the organization or elsewhere)?

SAMPLE INTERVIEW FORM

Conducted by: _____

Date: _____

Job Title: _____   Immediate Supervisor: _____

Incumbent's Name: _____

Department: _____   Length of time in job: _____

Division: _____

Duties Usually Performed   Approximate % of Time

Duties Occasionally Performed   Frequency

Most Complex or Difficult Duty Performed:

Qualifications: (experience, education, training, physical requirements, aptitudes, skills, etc.)

SAMPLE INTERVIEW FORM
(Nonexempt)

Job Title: _____   Department: _____

Incumbent: _____   Time in job: _____

Interviewer: _____   Date: _____

1. State the function of your job.

2. What are your principal activities, and to what or to whom do they relate?

3. Are you responsible for coaching, training, or following up on the work of other employees? Who are they?

4. How important is accuracy in your work? Who double-checks your work?

5. What do you feel is the most difficult or complicated part of your job? Why?

6. What kinds of problems or questions would you ordinarily refer to your supervisor?

7. What kinds of contacts do you have with others? Describe.

8. Give a brief analysis of how you spend your time (i.e., what tasks take what percentage of your time).

9. What qualifications do you feel are absolutely essential to perform this job successfully? Why?

SAMPLE INTERVIEW FORM
(Line Management)

Position Title: _____ **Date:** _____

Incumbent: _____ **Dept.:** _____

Interviewer: _____

1. ACCOUNTABILITY:
   To whom do you report?

   For what are you accountable?

2. OPERATIONS: Describe the operations or processes for which you are responsible.

3. EQUIPMENT: List the equipment or machines utilized. Give receiving or shipping statistics, where applicable.

4. SCHEDULES: Describe your responsibility for scheduling (products, operations, manpower, etc.).

5. SPECIFICATIONS AND CONTROLS: List the specifications and controls within which operations are conducted.

6. CONTACTS: List your most frequent contacts—with whom and why

    Internal

    External

7. SUPERVISION: Describe your supervisory responsibilities in terms of the following—
    Number of people supervised (salaried, hourly); their job titles

    Nature of supervision (close, frequent; occasional, when needed; constant, etc.)

    Are there fluctuations in your supervisory activities (certain periods when they require more of your time, etc.)?

8. PRINCIPAL ACTIVITIES: Describe what you do in the following areas—
Work assignments

Instruction/training/coaching

Follow-up/follow-through

Discipline

Grievance handling

Hiring/placement

Performance appraisal

Troubleshooting

Work or material flow

Developing new products or patterns

Quality control/improvement

Cost reduction

Incentives

Methods

Reports

Other

9. JUDGMENTS AND RECOMMENDATIONS: List the most important judgments that fall within your authority; also list important recommendations made for approval by others.

10. Give an approximate breakdown of how you spend your time; list major duties or activities and percentage of time devoted to each.

11. Other relevant comments:

QUESTIONNAIRES

For most companies, this is probably the least costly method for collecting job analysis information. A well-designed questionnaire enables the analyst to gather a wide array of job information in a relatively short period of time. Questionnaires are particularly useful when job analysis is being conducted on a large scale and individual interviews would be impractical. Skilled hourly positions and many clerical positions have been successfully analyzed on the basis of questionnaires.

There are, however, a few "golden rules" that should be followed in using this method:

1. The questionnaire should contain only questions that employees can relate to their own jobs. For example, a sales clerk's questionnaire may ask questions about writing sales slips and balancing a cash register, while a factory worker's questionnaire should ask questions about equipment used, tolerances permitted, and the type of supervision received. The more specific the questionnaire for a particular type of job is, the more useful the information is going to be.
2. The form should contain questions that are easily understood and that require only brief, factual answers. When using a questionnaire to solicit information about highly routine or repetitive jobs—or jobs about which an employee might have trouble expressing himself—it may be a good idea to develop a checklist of duties and ask as few open-ended questions as possible.
3. Employees should be asked to sign the questionnaire and have it approved by their supervisors to ensure that they have represented the position accurately. Some forms have a separate section for the supervisor's comments on the accuracy and completeness of the answers given. Significant omissions or additions should be explained here.

DEVELOPING THE QUESTIONNAIRE

The job analyst should visit the department where jobs are to be analyzed and review the positions to be studied. He or she should work closely with the supervisor(s) and the department head in developing the questionnaire, especially if the jobs have technical aspects with which the analyst is not familiar. The analyst should familiarize himself with the organization of the department and its reporting relationships.

Once a rough draft of the questionnaire has been prepared, the supervisor or department head should review it for any weaknesses or oversights. Once the final questionnaire is ready, the department head should meet with employees in the jobs to be studied to discuss the need for job analysis, how the questionnaire is to be completed, and to answer any questions the employees might have. It's a good idea to have a sample questionnaire to pass around the group so that employees know in advance what to expect.

When the questionnaires have been completed by the incumbents, they should be reviewed by the supervisor or department head for accuracy. Any additions or corrections should be discussed with the employee and made with his or her approval. The questionnaires are then sent back to the analyst for a final review of the information provided.

PROS AND CONS OF QUESTIONNAIRES

Questionnaires are particularly useful in analyzing high-level positions, where incumbents are usually more skilled in written expression than at lower levels of the company. But they have also proved successful in analyzing routine, repetitive jobs where duties and responsibilities can be spelled out fairly simply in written form. In short, the success of this method rests with the design of the questionnaire form and the individuals who are asked to fill it out. Its biggest advantage is that it saves a great deal of time for the analyst, who does not have to engage in lengthy observations or individual interviews.

But questionnaires have their drawbacks, among them the following:
- While they may save time for the analyst, they can be extremely time-consuming for the employee and/or supervisor to fill out.
- They do not allow the analyst any formal contact with the jobholder.
- Many employees are simply not trained to express themselves and describe their jobs in writing.
- Respondents have a tendency to go to one extreme or the other, giving answers that are either too sketchy or too long.
- For some types of jobs, it can be very difficult to design a questionnaire that will elicit the desired information.

Perhaps the biggest drawback of all is the fact that many people simply dislike filling out forms. They may consider job analysis questionnaires a waste of time and effort, if not an invasion of privacy. The key here is to convince the jobholder ahead of time that complete and accurate answers to the questions are vital to his or her well-being and future in the company.

As with most other job analysis techniques that rely on what the incumbent has to say about the job, there is always the problem of "job inflation" as well. This is what happens when an employee consciously or unconsciously distorts his or her description of job tasks or responsibilities. She may exaggerate the amount of time spent on tasks she enjoys—or, conversely, underestimate the time spent on enjoyable tasks because they do not seem as burdensome. Another form of job inflation occurs when the incumbent identifies his personal qualifications with the necessary qualifications for the job. He may say that a college education is required simply because *he* attended four years of college, when in reality a high school diploma and on-the-job training are all that is really necessary. There is always a tendency among incumbents to try to impress the job analyst in the hope that it will lead to a higher wage and salary classification, a more prestigious title, or simply more attention from management. Observation or interviews can be used to double-check questionnaire responses, but this is going to mean that the time-saving advantage is lost. Another means of counteracting job inflation is to compare the responses of a large number of incumbents within the same job classification. Instances where an individual has altered the facts to suit his self-image or career goals will usually become obvious.

The sample questionnaires on the pages that follow are directed at a variety of job levels. Remember that questionnaires must be aimed specifically at the type of job you are analyzing. Some of the sample forms here are more "general" than others.

SAMPLE QUESTIONNAIRE

EMPLOYEE'S NAME _____   DATE _____

POSITION TITLE _____   DEPARTMENT _____

SUPERVISOR'S NAME _____   SUPERVISOR'S TITLE _____

INSTRUCTIONS

EMPLOYEE: Complete Section I. Describe in detail the primary or most important duties that you as an employee perform. List the job duties in clear, concise sentences. Indicate the frequency (day, week, month) and amount of time spent performing these primary job duties. Be certain that you provide sufficient information about each specific duty to enable persons unfamiliar with your work to understand what the duty entails. Questions should be directed to your supervisor.

SUPERVISOR: Complete Section II.

SECTION I

1. Duty (what) _____
   Procedure (how) _____
   _____
   _____
   Reason for duty (why) _____
   _____
   Frequency _____ and Percentage _____ of time spent performing above duty.

2. Duty (what) _____
   Procedure (how) _____
   _____
   _____
   Reason for duty (why) _____
   _____
   Frequency _____ and Percentage _____ of time spent performing above duty.

3. Duty (what) _____
   Procedure (how) _____
   _____
   _____
   Reason for duty (why) _____
   _____
   Frequency_____ and Percentage_____ of time spent performing above duty.

4. Duty (what) _____
   Procedure (how) _____
   _____
   _____
   Reason for duty (why) _____
   _____
   Frequency_____ and Percentage _____ of time spent performing above duty.

5. Duty (what) _____
   Procedure (how) _____
   _____
   _____
   Reason for duty (why) _____
   _____
   Frequency_____ and Percentage_____ of time spent performing above duty.

6. Duty (what) _____
   Procedure (how) _____
   _____
   _____
   Reason for duty (why) _____
   _____
   Frequency_____ and Percentage_____ of time spent performing above duty.

What machines/equipment are you required to use proficiently on your job? How much time per day or week is spent using each machine/equipment listed?

Machine/Equipment	Time in Use
_____	_____
_____	_____
_____	_____

What are the most difficult decisions you make? What do you consider the most important task(s) you perform?

_____
_____
_____
_____

Describe the working conditions which may cause a feeling of pressure or discomfort. Consider environment, distractions and interference which might make completion of task(s) difficult:

_____
_____
_____
_____

Describe the personal contacts you are required to make to perform the job.

Who (Title?) _____   Reason _____

Who (Title?) _____   Reason _____

Who (Title?) _____   Reason _____

Signature _____
(Employee)

SECTION II

Section I reviewed and approved by _____
                                                      (Immediate Supervisor)

Comments: _____
_____
_____
_____
_____
_____
_____

Errors which may occur in performance of this job are: (Check one)
___ *easily detected in normal routine of checking results.*
___ *detected in subsequent steps.*
    Give example: _____
___ *not detected until they have caused other departments considerable inconvenience.*
    Give example: _____
___ *not detected until they have caused considerable inconvenience to another company.*
    Give example: _____

Describe responsibility of the occupant of this position for work of other employees. (Check one)
___ *No responsibility for work of others. May show other employees how to perform a task or assist in indoctrination of new employees.*
___ *Guides and instructs other employees, assigning, checking, and maintaining the flow of work.*

SAMPLE QUESTIONNAIRE
(Maintenance Worker)

Instructions: As part of our job analysis program, we are asking you to complete this questionnaire describing your job. To help you cover all the important points, we have included a number of specific questions about exactly what you do. Try to be clear, concise, and straightforward in your answers.

Your Name: _____   Date: _____

Job Title: _____   Department: _____

Supervisor's Name: _____   His/Her Title: _____

1. What do you do?
   —List the equipment and assemblies you repair. If possible, give examples of typical repair jobs for each.

   —List your other maintenance tasks.

   —List the tools and equipment you use.

2. To what extent is your work supervised?
—How do you receive instruction?

—Do you have to read and use blueprints, instruction manuals, or other written materials? If so, explain.

—How often does your supervisor check your work?

3. Do you supervise other workers? If so, list their job titles and explain briefly the nature of your supervisory duties.

4. If you think there are other relevant facts we should know about your job, describe them briefly below.

_____
Employee's Signature

_____
Supervisor's Signature

SAMPLE QUESTIONNAIRE
(Exempt Positions)

Instructions: This is a preliminary step in the preparation of a position description for your job. Complete the questionnaire carefully and give it to your immediate superior to review. He or she will then pass it on to the analyst responsible for your area. Use the back of the page if there is not sufficient space for your answers, but try to keep them as concise and relevant as possible.

Your Name: _____ **Date:** _____

Job Title: _____ **Department:** _____

Immediate Superior: _____ **His/Her Title:** _____

1. How would you describe the primary purpose of your job? (i.e., why does it exist?)

2. What is the position immediately superior to yours?

3. List the titles of the jobs you supervise or direct and the number of incumbents in each. Briefly describe the nature of your supervisory activities.

4. What kind of supervision or direction do you receive (if any)? (for example, to whom you report, from whom you receive assignments, etc.)

5. What procedural controls are you subject to? (e.g., sales goals, budgets, cost standards, etc.)

6. What are the positions or departments with which you have close working relationships and frequent contacts? What is the nature of these contacts?

7. Describe your major job activities (include planning, scheduling, coordinating, etc.).

8. For what dollar amounts are you accountable? (e.g., department operating costs, approximate size of payroll supervised, money spent, sales made, etc.)

9. Describe anything else you feel is applicable to the position that is not covered above.

10. List the qualifications (in terms of education, experience, training, etc.) you feel are crucial to the position.

```
                                              _____
                                                   Your Signature
                              Approved by:    _____
                                                 Superior's Signature

                                              _____
                                                       Date
```

DIARY/LOG

The diary or log technique isn't as widely used as the interview, observation, and questionnaire. While it is obviously a time-saver for the analyst, it can be time-consuming for the employee to the point where it actually interferes with the performance of job duties. It can be difficult for the employee to maintain a complete log if constant interruptions (phone calls, etc.) are a regular part of the job.

Another drawback of this method is that employees tend to identify it with a "time and motion" study. They may feel they are being put on the spot about the way they spend their time, and may even be tempted to "cheat" a little on the log to make it reflect the way they *think* management wants them to spend their time.

Like the questionnaire, the diary/log approach does not allow for much contact between the job analyst and employees. But this problem can be overcome by having the analyst meet with employees prior to the time they are asked to maintain a log. He or she can then explain the purpose of the log, pass around some sample logs that have been kept for similar type jobs, and answer any questions. Most important of all, the analyst can stress the point that this is a job analysis—not a time and motion study.

At the end of the day, the employee should review the diary or log and mentally compare it with the day's activities. It should also contain sections for recording activities that are performed at irregular or infrequent intervals. The diary/log method is most widely used for jobs at one end or the other of the organizational hierarchy: for routine, repetitive jobs or for jobs requiring a high degree of technical or scientific knowledge.

A portable tape recorder can facilitate the use of this method. The jobholder can "talk through" his activities as he performs them. The job analyst can then transcribe the tape.

INNOVATIONS IN JOB ANALYSIS TECHNIQUES

The conventional approaches to job analysis discussed above have proved their usefulness in a wide variety of organizational contexts. They do, however, have their limitations—most of which stem from their dependence on verbal material, either spoken or written. There is always the possibility that something will be lost or misunderstood in conveying the intended meaning.

To counter this weakness in conventional techniques, there have been a number of attempts over the years to develop more systematic, scientific job analysis methods, with an emphasis on quantitative rather than qualitative responses. These efforts have focused on developing techniques to identify and/or measure units of job-related information (such as tasks or worker attributes) that make it possible to compare and group jobs more easily and that make job-related information in general more usable. They are known as "structured" job analysis procedures.

Most of these structured approaches were not designed with the intention of replacing conventional job analysis methods altogether. The idea has been to develop methods that can serve certain purposes better, or that serve purposes that can't be served by conventional approaches. Some job analysis programs combine conventional and structured methods. Several of the more widely used innovations in job analysis methods are discussed briefly below.

FUNCTIONAL JOB ANALYSIS

This technique makes use of the three worker function hierarchies (data, people, and things) used by the *Dictionary of Occupational Titles* in assigning numerical codes to various jobs. Functional job analysis (FJA) is both a system for defining the dimensions of worker activity and a method of measuring levels of worker activity. According to Dr. Sidney Fine, who helped formulate the method, its basic premises are as follows:

1. A fundamental distinction must be made between *what gets done* and *what workers do* to get things done. (For example, the bus driver doesn't carry passengers; what he does is perform a number of sequenced tasks to drive a vehicle and collect fares.)
2. What workers do, as far as their job context is concerned, they do in relation to three so-called "primitives": data, people, and things.
3. Workers function in unique ways in relation to each of these primitives. In relation to things, they draw upon physical resources; in relation to data, on mental resources; and in relation to people, on interpersonal resources.
4. All jobs require the worker to relate to each of these primitives in some degree.
5. Although the behavior of workers or the tasks they perform can apparently be described in an infinite number of ways, there are only a few definitive functions involved. In interacting with machines, for example, workers feed, tend, operate, or set up. Although each of these functions occurs over a range of difficulty and context, essentially each draws on a relatively narrow and specific range of similar worker characteristics and qualifications for effective performance.
6. The functions appropriate to each primitive can be arranged along a hierarchical scale, proceeding from the simple to the complex. The FJA system provides for the analysis of jobs in terms of the *level* and *orientation* of involvement with the three hierarchies.

Without getting unnecessarily bogged down in the details of the FJA system, it can readily be seen that by identifying and categorizing various aspects of jobs in terms of their relationship to data, people, and things, each job can be rated and thus compared to other jobs in the organization without depending on the largely subjective account of job duties provided by the incumbent under a more conventional system.

TASK INVENTORIES

A task inventory consists of two basic features: a list of tasks for the occupational field in question, and some type of response scale for each task. The list of tasks usually covers most (if not all) of the tasks that can be performed by incumbents within the occupational field; each is presented in the form of a short statement of *what* is done (not how or why). The response scale might indicate the importance of the task to the job, the frequency of performance, the time spent on the task (either in terms of minutes or relative to time spent on other tasks) or some other "primary rating factor." A second type of response scale ("secondary rating factors") indicates the complexity or criticalness of the task, the difficulty of learning it, the amount of training required for the task, the difficulty of performing it, the supervision required, or some other type of basically subjective response. The end results of task inventories are typically expressed in quantitative terms as related to specific tasks and do not provide an integrated picture of the job.

Data from task inventories are particularly useful for identifying job types or planning training programs. However, they are not as effective in serving other purposes. Because the development of a task inventory is so time-consuming, and can be justified only if the number of incumbents warrants the effort, many firms prefer to locate a task inventory that has already been developed for the occupational field in question and that can be used either as is or with any minor modifications.

CRITICAL INCIDENT TECHNIQUE

As an approach to job analysis, the critical incident technique involves the recording of job-related behaviors that are critical to job performance and that reflect either highly effective (or successful) behavior or very ineffective (or unsuccessful) behavior on the part of the incumbent. In other words, the job incumbent (or his supervisor, or an impartial observer) writes down examples of very good or very poor job behavior as they occur, or recalls such events as they have occurred in the past. This written record should contain the following information about each incident:

- What led up to the incident;
- What the employee did;
- The consequences (either actual or implied) of the behavior;
- Whether or not these consequences were within the employee's control.

It is usually necessary to obtain hundreds or even thousands of critical incidents for job analysis purposes. These are then categorized by either the job analyst or (ideally) by a panel of judges into reasonably homogeneous groups or "dimensions" on the basis of the type of behavior implied. Eventually all (or almost all) of the incidents should be allocated into one of these categories and each should be named and carefully defined with a brief descriptive paragraph. For example, one of the dimensions of behavior for the job of clerk-typist might be the "ability to work accurately and neatly." The critical incidents in this category might be described as follows:

1. Notices an item in a report that didn't appear to be right, checks it, and corrects the error.
2. Notices an incorrect address on a mailing list and corrects it.
3. Uses a style manual when a question arises concerning proper usage.
4. Misfiles letters frequently.
5. Types important information incorrectly due to carelessness.
6. Fails to use the dictionary "when in doubt" about the spelling of a word.
7. Makes typing errors and incorrect margins that necessitate the retyping of a 500-page report.

The various dimensions for a particular job are then rated on the basis of their criticalness or importance to the job, using a scale similar to the following:

1 Extremely important
2 Very important
3 Important
4 Only slightly important
5 Hardly important at all

The mean rating of a number of judges can then be used to rank each of the dimensions identified for the job.

The critical incident technique is especially useful as a performance appraisal procedure. However, the data on critical incidents accumulated for a number of incumbents can also be used to analyze the job, especially the human qualities or attributes required for successful performance. Other possible uses include identifying training needs, developing work sample tests, and vocational counseling.

POSITION ANALYSIS QUESTIONNAIRE (PAQ)

This is one of the most sophisticated and yet easily administered techniques. It consists of a standard form that takes about two hours to complete (which may be a drawback), is easily scored, and is applicable to a wide variety of jobs. The PAQ analyzes jobs in terms of 187 job elements. These elements are of a worker-oriented nature, meaning that they characterize or imply the human behaviors that are involved in various jobs. They are organized into six groups as follows:

(1) **Information input:** Where and how does the worker get the information he or she uses in performing the job?
(2) **Mental processes:** What reasoning, decision-making, planning, and

information-processing activities are involved in performing the job?

(3) **Work output:** What physical activities does the worker perform and what tools or devices does he/she use?

(4) **Relationships with other persons:** What relationships with other people are required in performing the job?

(5) **Job context:** In what physical or social context(s) is the work performed?

(6) **Other job characteristics:** What activities, conditions, or characteristics other than those described above are relevant to the job?

A specific rating scale is designated to be used with each job element, according to which of the six PAQ rating scales is most appropriate: (1) extent of use; (2) importance to the job; (3) amount of time; (4) possibility of occurrence; (5) applicability; and (6) special code, used in the case of a few specific job elements.

The analysis of jobs with the PAQ is usually carried out by job analysts, personnel staffers, or supervisors. But in some cases job incumbents are asked to analyze their own jobs—especially in the case of managerial, professional, and other white-collar positions.

THE HAY SYSTEM

Devised by Hay and Associates, this is a widely known and used approach to job analysis, especially when it is linked to wage and salary administration. The Hay System measures each job in terms of three factors: know-how, problem solving, and accountability. A fourth factor, working conditions, is introduced for certain jobs subject to extreme hazards or strenuous work. The three basic job elements are defined as follows:

1. **Know-how** is the sum total of all knowledge and skills, however acquired, which are needed for satisfactory job performance.
2. **Problem solving** is the amount of original, self-starting thinking required by the job for analyzing, evaluating, creating, reasoning, and arriving at conclusions.
3. **Accountability** is the degree to which an incumbent is answerable for his/her actions and for the consequences of these actions.

Because the Hay System is known primarily as a technique for job evaluation, we will not discuss the details of how each of these three elements is rated. But it is important to note that the Hay System depends heavily upon written job descriptions. If your company is undertaking job analysis in order to improve or update job descriptions, the Hay System is not going to solve your problems. Because a thorough understanding of the jobs is basic to the entire system, it is usually assumed that the company planning on using Hay already has a meaningful, accurate, and up-to-date set of job descriptions.

JOB INFORMATION MATRIX SYSTEM (JIMS)

Another approach to providing job information is known as the Job Information Matrix System, developed by Stone and Yoder and their associates. It provides a standardized basis for gathering and recording job information in the following categories:

1. What the worker *does*
2. What the worker *uses*
3. What *knowledge* the worker must have
4. The worker's *responsibilities*
5. The *working conditions* of the job

For each of these categories of information the JIMS provides "modules" or "units" of information to be used in the analysis of jobs. The JIMS procedure must be tailored to specific occupational areas. In fact, it has been applied to the machining area with promising results. But it is not a "complete" system in the sense that certain features of it have yet to be developed with respect to specific occupational areas.

The JIMS can normally be used by supervisors or others who are thoroughly familiar with the job in question, including the workers themselves. Although a job analyst would still be needed, his or her function would basically be to monitor the analyses performed by others. The JIMS lends itself quite readily to computer storage and retrieval of job data; but in its present form it should probably be regarded as a "demonstration" approach to job analysis.

JOB ELEMENT METHOD

The Job Element Method was developed by Dr. Ernest Primoff of the United States Civil Service Commission for establishing selection standards for federal government jobs. What he calls "job elements" are the various types of knowledge, abilities, skills, and personal characteristics that determine success in jobs. Some examples would be "Estimate size of objects," "Arithmetic computation," and "Oral expression." Job supervisors and "expert" employees analyze the jobs in terms of these elements, using a simple 3-point scale:

0 **The element is not present in the job.**
1 **The element is present in the job, but not of extreme importance.**
2 **The element is present and of extreme importance to the job.**

The value of a given element is the sum of the ratings (0, 1, or 2 points respectively) given by these individuals. These values then serve as the basis for estimating the validity of one or more standardized tests for use in personnel selection.

OCCUPATIONAL ANALYSIS INVENTORY (OAI)

The OAI represents an approach similar to that of the Position Analysis Questionnaire. It consists of 622 work elements grouped into five categories: (1) information received; (2) mental activities; (3) work behavior; (4) work goals; and (5) work context. Many of these work elements are identical to or similar to the job elements of the PAQ. Both techniques deal with information input, mental processes, and work output. But the OAI incorporates many job-oriented work elements, while the PAQ has only worker-oriented elements. A second distinguishing feature of the OAI is that it incorporates work elements dealing with work goals, such as "electronic devices installed or assembled."

The work elements of the OAI are generally rated on three standard scales: "significance to the job," "extent of occurrence," and "applicability." Some of the work elements have special rating scales.

COMPENSABLE FACTORS

In this brief discussion of some of the structured approaches to job analysis, you may have noticed that terms like "job elements" and "dimensions" of job behavior seem to crop up with regularity. What most job analysis methods are trying to define is the factors that are common among jobs to a greater or lesser extent. Job analysis makes it possible not only to identify but to define and weigh these "compensable factors," which are the basic criteria upon which the relative assessment of the job is based. The functions and requirements of the various jobs within an organization determine the choice of compensable factors for job analysis purposes. In fact, the failure of job analysis—and the inadequacy of the resulting job descriptions—can in most cases be traced to the inability of the job analyst to pinpoint these compensable factors.

Because compensable factors are usually found in the context of a job evaluation program, we will not discuss them in detail in this book. (For a detailed analysis, see *Job Evaluations and Job Pricing*, also published by BLB.) But they can serve a host of other organizational needs, including performance appraisal, selection and placement, and training. We mention compensable factors here because the attempt to pinpoint them is what most structured approaches to job analysis have in common, and because the objectivity and accuracy with which they are developed can make or break any job analysis program.

WHY ARE SO MANY COMPANIES DISSATISFIED WITH JOB ANALYSIS?

Despite the wide variety of job analysis techniques, both conventional and structured, many firms either do not have job analysis programs or are dissatisfied with the results of their program. A recent survey carried out by the Bureau of Business Research at California State College revealed that the reasons most commonly given by organizations for *not* having job analysis programs were as follows:

(1) It would serve no useful purpose.
(2) An acceptable system has not been found.
(3) It's too expensive.
(4) It takes too much time.

The survey summarizes the respondents' dissatisfactions by pointing out that "the traditional methods of gathering job information are time consuming and difficult to perform with anything more than a modicum of consistency and currency. As a result, necessary updating of job information often proves costly and impractical." Another shortcoming of traditional methods pointed out by the survey's authors (Jones and DeCoths) is that their subjective and narrative nature limits their adaptability to automation and computerization. Dissatisfaction has also focused on the difficulty of adapting a common job analysis method for diverse purposes. Many job analysis programs simply lack the sophistication demanded by such purposes as the construction of vocational tests, the development of training courses, and job restructuring.

The authors say that a great deal of this dissatisfaction can be attributed to the lack of standardized, quantifiable techniques for gathering, recording and presenting job information. Some of the more recent structured approaches to job analysis have attempted to redress these shortcomings. In addition, most job analysis programs are characterized by relatively little emphasis on human relations type job variables, which are more difficult to identify and rate.

The comparable worth issue has focused attention on the need to quantify job information, increase its validity, and eliminate its subjectiveness. In fact, the pressures brought to bear on employers by not only women but minorities and the underemployed have given a real boost to the "scientific" trend in job analysis techniques. There appears to be good reason to expect that some of the more structured approaches to job analysis presented here will gain wider acceptance or will be modified for wider use in the near future.

HOW TO ORDER MORE COPIES OF THIS BOOK

How Many People in Your Organization Should Be Reading This Book?

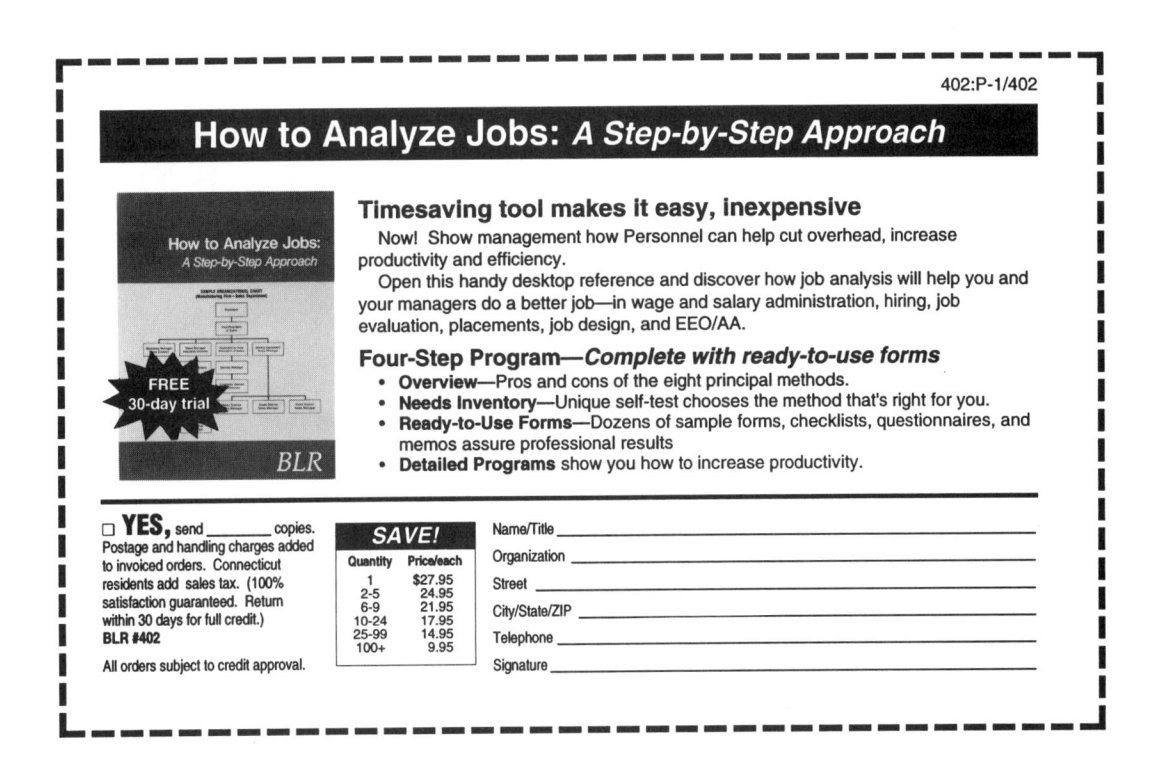

402:P-1/402

How to Analyze Jobs: *A Step-by-Step Approach*

Timesaving tool makes it easy, inexpensive

Now! Show management how Personnel can help cut overhead, increase productivity and efficiency.

Open this handy desktop reference and discover how job analysis will help you and your managers do a better job—in wage and salary administration, hiring, job evaluation, placements, job design, and EEO/AA.

Four-Step Program—*Complete with ready-to-use forms*
- **Overview**—Pros and cons of the eight principal methods.
- **Needs Inventory**—Unique self-test chooses the method that's right for you.
- **Ready-to-Use Forms**—Dozens of sample forms, checklists, questionnaires, and memos assure professional results
- **Detailed Programs** show you how to increase productivity.

☐ **YES,** send _____ copies. Postage and handling charges added to invoiced orders. Connecticut residents add sales tax. (100% satisfaction guaranteed. Return within 30 days for full credit.)
BLR #402

All orders subject to credit approval.

SAVE!

Quantity	Price/each
1	$27.95
2-5	24.95
6-9	21.95
10-24	17.95
25-99	14.95
100+	9.95

Name/Title _____
Organization _____
Street _____
City/State/ZIP _____
Telephone _____
Signature _____

FREE 30-day trial

Copy (to avoid tearing page) and Mail or FAX to:

BUSINESS & LEGAL REPORTS, INC.
39 Academy Street • Madison, CT 06443-1513
FAX (203) 245-2559